inevitable

Mass Customized Learning
Learning in the Age of Empowerment

Chuck Schwahn & Bea McGarvey

ISBN: 1470059053
ISBN-13: 9781470059057

Table of Contents

Introduction

*"At first, dreams seem impossible, then improbable,
and eventually........inevitable."*

Christopher Reeve

*"At every crossway on the road that leads to the future,
each progressive spirit is opposed
by a thousand men appointed to guard the past."*

**Maurice Maeterlinck
Belgian Nobel Laureate in Literature**

*"Optimists enrich the present, enhance the future,
challenge the improbable, and attain the impossible."*

William Arthur

Why the Title "Inevitable?"

The world is changing . . . no, excuse us, it's not changing, it already has changed! We have left the Industrial Age and mass production and seen our way into, and maybe past, the Information Age and mass customization. Except for education, of course . . . which remains stuck in the assembly line approach to education which presupposes that all eight-year olds are ready to learn the same thing, the same way, in the same amount of time. Soooo 20th century!

The forces *demanding* that education change are many and powerful; and the forces *resisting* educational transformation are also many and powerful. But the *future* will win out because:

☑ Reality is that no one (other than those who have that lovely second grade teacher for their child) believes that public schools are doing a good job of preparing our students for the future. The US is near the bottom of almost all rankings of achievement when compared with other developed countries. (More about this in Chapter 1.)

☑ Technology is transforming nearly every sector of our lives. Music, books, retailing, communication, news, photography, medicine, architecture, etc. etc. etc. have changed drastically, have become more efficient, and we all expect that those changes, improvements, and progress will continue. Education cannot sit in this customized world as an island, embracing the Industrial Age, and expect

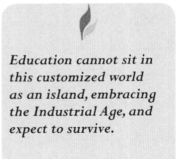

Education cannot sit in this customized world as an island, embracing the Industrial Age, and expect to survive.

to survive. The only question is: will "they" do it, or will "we" do it? Educational change, though difficult, is inevitable. (More about this in Chapter 2.)

☑ Mass Customizing models are out there. They are everywhere. We are all using them. . . .without ever once stopping to reflect on how this technology and these strategies could/should be applied to learning and learners. Think iTunes and music, think Amazon and book sales, think Verizon and your phone bill, think eBay and your garage sale . . . just start watching the mass customizing that you are experiencing each day and you will learn firsthand that the technology needed to transform, to personalize and customize learning, is already available. (More about this in Chapter 8.)

☑ Customizing and personalizing learning to the individual learner will allow educators to move from "workers" to professionals, and allow education to move from an "industry" to a profession. Clear and comprehensive definitions of "professionalism" and "professions" would not allow the inclusion of today's Industrial Age schools. (More about this in Chapter 5.)

☑ Customizing and personalizing learning can be done without increasing the cost of education. This statement may make us sound like politicians, but songs are cheaper than ever, Kindle has made books cheaper than ever, long-distance calls are cheaper than ever . . . and we could go on and on. Transformational technologies have decreased costs nearly everywhere. We are not trying to sell MASS CUSTOMIZED LEARNING (**MCL**) as a cost cutter, but neither do we want to lose the debate for educational reform over co$ts.

Why the Book?

Now that you know why we chose Inevitable as our title, let us be up-front about why we thought that this book needed to be written. We believe that making education more meaningful to learners, making learning more motivational for learners, and preparing young learners for their future rather than our past is the critical educational and moral (not to mention – economic) imperative of the day.

We have walked by too many open high school classroom doors at 11 am and 2 pm, looked at students sitting in rows, listening but not hearing what teachers were saying, telling us with their posture and their eyes how they felt. We have watched too many enthusiastic first graders turn into bored fourth graders. We are morally compelled to make things better for learners, for teachers, and for the system that we refer to as "having school." But more specifically, we wrote _Inevitable_:

▶ To enthusiastically and passionately promote a vision of education that is intrinsically motivating to young learners.

▶ To create a concrete vision of an Information Age instructional delivery system to replace the present and severely outdated Industrial Age bureaucracy.

▶ To begin a focused dialogue about the opportunity educators have to make education significantly more exciting and effective.

▶ To help move public education from an industry to a profession.

▶ In short, to bring education into the 21st century.

Note: Before we/you get too far into _Inevitable: Mass Customized Learning_, we want to be clear that this is not a book about cyber schools. It is not about technology as teacher. It is about technology as enabler. About technology that "enables" professional educators to implement the most basic research we have regarding learners and learning, and teachers and teaching.

> .....that this is not a book about cyber schools. It is not about technology as teacher. It is about technology as enabler.

Our Intended Audience

Public education is difficult to change. (That line will easily win the "understatement award" for this entire book.) Our experiences cause us to think that education IS the most difficult of all industries/professions to change in any significant and fundamental way. Given education's resistance to meaningful change, it is critical that all stakeholder groups work together supporting a common vision if meaningful change is to occur. So, _Inevitable_ is not a book for educators and educational leaders.

Oh, we want them too, of course; that is for sure. But we also want _Inevitable_ to be read by parents, board members, community members, business people, taxpayers, and ALSO by students. No, please excuse us again, that should read "ESPECIALLY" by students.

If we can convince the "born digital" group (those born after 1990 by our definition) that we are serious about transforming schools, we might expect that the born digitals will tell us how to do it . . . oops again, we can expect the digital natives to "show" us digital immigrants how to do it. If you don't understand this paragraph and you have a 12-year old in the house, just go ask. Digital natives live their lives where we will be asking schools to go . . . except for their school life, of course. As one insightful high schooler put it, "I have to "power down" when I go to school." We fully expect that today's middle schoolers will "get" the concept/vision of **MCL** before their digital immigrant parents and teachers do.

With the need for total cooperation and support in mind, we will attempt to write in a style that is inclusive, conversational, informal, and fun. But because our topic requires authenticity, openness, and candor, we will also be confrontational and challenging. We believe that the need to transform education is so critical that it cannot be political. We need everyone . . . we will attempt to be "equal opportunity" offenders when we confront and challenge.

Our Perspective

The reader should know our vantage point going in. We are lifelong educators (although we also frequently consult with businesses and other professions) and lifelong learners who believe that education is the world's most important profession. Nothing is more meaningful than to play a critical role in the life and learning of a young girl or boy, or a young woman or young man. Nothing is more meaningful than *empowering all learners to succeed in a rapidly changing world.*

Together, we (Chuck and Bea) have about 90 years of experience as educators, have sat in almost every chair on the organizational chart, and have been successful in nearly everything to which we have committed (said Chuck and Bea boastfully). "Helping People Grow" is our personal and professional mission. We are perennial and resilient optimists who are passionate about our profession.

Our core values *which guide our thoughts,* *decisions, and actions* *are:* *People and Relationships,* *Honesty and Integrity,* *Freedom and Responsibility, and* *Continuous Learning.*	*Our* principles of professionalism *which provide rules for decisions* *and performance include:* *Client Centeredness,* *Future-Focusing,* *Inclusiveness,* *Inquiry, Contribution,* *Accountability, and* *Win-Win Thinking.*

We do have biases . . . as does everyone, we have points of view, and we do take positions on most big issues of the day. Some of those biases may leak through as we discuss our vision for education in a clear and passionate manner. But, know that we will do our best to remain neutral on those things not pertinent to *Inevitable: Mass Customized Learning*.

Our experiences have taught us to take no prisoners. We know that we can't change the minds of some people, and so when we feel a hint of deep defensiveness, we move on. Our role, and the purpose of _Inevitable_, is not to change the heart and soul of anyone. Rather, our purpose and the purpose of _Inevitable_ is to give those who know that we can do better, and who want to be part of the journey, **a place to go**.

If you are ready for a challenging and transformational MASS CUSTOMIZED LEARNING (**MCL**) vision, hop in. And oh yes, it might be good if you fasten that seatbelt!

Chapter 1
Facing Reality

*"The first critical job of a leader is
to identify and to face reality."*

*"You must never confuse
faith that you will prevail in the end
(which you can never afford to lose)
with the discipline to confront
the most brutal facts of your current reality,
whatever they might be."*

Jim Collins in _Good to Great_

Authors write with intent. We want something of you, the reader. We want to do something with your thinking. In our bold spirit of transparency, we have chosen to tell you what we are trying to do with your thinking at the beginning of each chapter. And just so you know, when you finish this book, our intent is that you become "Raving Fans" of MASS CUSTOMIZED LEARNING.

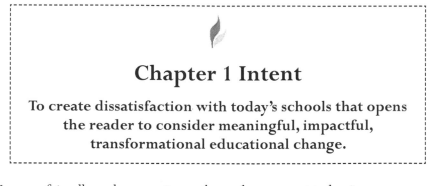

Chapter 1 Intent

To create dissatisfaction with today's schools that opens the reader to consider meaningful, impactful, transformational educational change.

We, your friendly and supportive authors, do not want to begin our very positive, exciting, and hopeful vision for education by making you, the reader, defensive. Education and educators have taken some pretty tough shots from nearly all sides over the past 20 years and we don't intend to "pile on." But, real and significant change begins with the title of Chapter 1, "Facing Reality," and we will not sugarcoat that reality.

We will do our very best to describe today's educational realities in a manner that does not cause anyone to feel defensive. We will be as objective as possible with our descriptions, our analyses, and our judgments . . . as we believe that the facts pretty well speak for themselves. We will not place blame or knock anyone . . . because we don't believe that anyone is to blame. On the other side of the coin, we expect that before finishing *Inevitable* you will want to accept today's realities so that we (all partners in education) will enthusiastically embrace a modern approach to education that motivates and meets personal learner needs every hour of every day.

To aid our analysis of major changes, of paradigm shifts – in this case, major changes in education – let us revisit the 1969 classic book *On Death And Dying* by Elizabeth Kubler-Ross. Kubler-Ross wrote about real death and dying, just as the title of her work would indicate. But since that time, her five stages of death and dying have been found by leadership and change theorists to help us understand any major change an individual, a group, or a society goes through.

The following five stages of loss – whether it be life itself, or the loss of a traditional way of doing things – seem to be common to the experience. We will present a quick example of the stages of death and dying . . . like "real death," and then we will present the stages providing examples related to being asked/forced to leave the security of the Industrial Age assembly line delivery of instruction for a delivery system personalized to each learner. (Much more about this shift throughout the remainder of the book.)

Stages of Death and Dying (taking some liberties with Ms. Kubler-Ross' work)	**Stages of the Change Process**
Stage 1: DENIAL "This can't be. That test isn't fool-proof, and it might have gotten messed up in the lab. I will need a second opinion. Gee, I feel so good!"	**Stage 1: DENIAL** "The parents of my students like me and like this school. We have always done it this way and the United States is still top dog. Those other countries don't test all of their kids so how can you compare test scores."
Stage 2: ANGER "Why me!!! I don't deserve this. I'm down to six cigarettes a day and my friends who do a pack a day seem to be getting along well. Why hasn't the AMA found a cure for this... they get all the money they want for research."	**Stage 2: ANGER** "Those people who do the loudest complaining have never been in a classroom with today's kids. Our student/teacher ratio continues to grow and we work long hours for low pay. Parents don't support us... when something goes wrong, they take the kid's side. Boy, it wasn't like that when I was a kid."
Stage 3: BARGAINING "OK, I'll stop smoking and lose 20 pounds. Do some charity work and maybe get back to going to Mass regularly. Maybe a trip to Mayo would assure me that I am doing all that I can."	**Stage 3: BARGAINING** "We need a computer lab so that we can take our classes down there a couple of times a week. And let's adopt the Differentiated Classroom program. That will help us meet the individual needs of young learners. Maybe we should try a block schedule."

Stages of Death and Dying (taking some liberties with Ms. Kubler-Ross' work)	Stages of the Change Process
Stage 4: DEPRESSION "Hell, it's no use. I can't beat those statistics... who am I kidding. Time to put my affairs in order, shut off the world, and let this thing take its course."	**Stage 4: DEPRESSION** "Nothing we do seems to make much difference and No Child Left Behind has us all focused on basic skills and testing. This is not why I got into education. Oh well, I only have four or five years left before I can take early retirement; maybe I can outlast this."
Stage 5: ACCEPTANCE "You know, this whole thing has taught me what's important in my life. I have some months and I want to make the most of them. I need to listen to Tim McGraw sing that "Live Like You Were Dying" song. How did it go now... 'I went sky diving, I went Rocky Mountain climbing, I spent 2.7 seconds on a bull name Fu Manchu...'"	**Stage 5: ACCEPTANCE** "I'm beginning to see where Mass Customized Learning makes sense. It would be a big change, but I think that it might be very rewarding... for students as well as us educators. It would be great if we had motivated learners and were able to use transformational technology to help us meet their learning needs on a daily basis. I'm ready to give MCL a serious look."

You may wish to stop for a time to reflect where you, your colleagues, and your friends are on this framework in regard to your acceptance of the need for education to change and your willingness to embrace that change. Kubler-Ross didn't suggest that we are in only one stage at a time. Like Abraham Maslow's Hierarchy of Needs, we most likely have one foot in one level/stage, and the other foot in the one above or the one below, and we sometimes move up the stages and sometimes down.

Our Present "Big Picture" Educational Realities

Time to recognize the "elephant in the room;" you know, the large animal that everyone knows is there but doesn't want to be the first to admit it or talk about it. Time to put "the moose on the table;" you know, that somewhat ugly thing that is not "politically correct" to discuss in sophisticated settings.

We begin defining today's reality with four rather in-your-face statements. Statements that are intended to begin a dialogue but not an argument. Once we begin to face these truths . . . without placing blame, we begin positioning ourselves, and our organization, to create meaningful and productive change.

Should you find/feel yourself becoming defensive, stop and get in touch with that defensiveness. Know that we too (Chuck and Bea) are lifetime educators. We believe very much in the power of learning -- and "helping people to grow" is our personal and professional mission in life. More about this later, but one of the reasons that no one is to blame for what we have today is that the technology to customize education to each learner has only been available to us for a short period of time. On the other side of the coin, there will be reason to place blame if we continue to resist significant change now that transformational technology is available to make **MCL** a reality.

Harsh Reality #1

No one thinks that we are doing a good job in preparing our students for a successful future.

Everyone . . . other than educators . . . is critical of our performance. (But not critical of Catholic Schools . . . who just happen to do Industrial Age schools better than anyone else.) The US ranks near the bottom of almost all international rankings. Authors who used to devote a chapter to the needs of education now dismiss us in a paragraph.

Harsh Reality #2

We are Industrial Age organizations existing in an Information Age world.

Our Industrial Age delivery system is an assembly line where time for learning is the constant and the quality of the learning is the variable.

Harsh Reality #3

We are bureaucratic monopolies existing in a world of customization and service.

Our policies and practices are chosen for "administrative convenience" and are inconsistent with our most basic research regarding the learning rates of students. Concern for the personal learning needs of students does not begin until students are assigned to a teacher and then only if the teacher chooses to personalize learning within a classroom setting.

Harsh Reality #4

We are an "industry" existing in a world that requires a profession.

We are union contract driven, controlled by outside forces, and seldom remove underperforming workers.

The above descriptions of today's public school realities may be a bit of an overgeneralization, but those able to be objective will agree that they are the norm of the day. But remember now, we are not blaming anyone. There is no one to blame. It simply is what is.

But then, you may not agree with our four reality statements. Let's check that out. How about applying the following scale to each of the four statements:

5 = You are so right on

4 = I want to agree, but you're making me angry

3 = Well, yes and no

2 = A few good points, but too negative

1 = You guys are communists

Your total score can range from 20 (you agree totally) to 5 (you agree very little). If your score for the four reality statements is:

18 to 20	You will enjoy this book because it will tell you and show you how to transform education/public schools.
15 to 17	Just because you got a bit angry with us doesn't mean that we can't be supportive colleagues.
12 to 14	Keep reading. We think you will change your mind somewhere near the middle of the book.

11 or below   You may wish to update your resume focusing on your high standards, classroom control, and lecturing skills. (Only kidding of course.) We think and believe that we will convince you of the validity of our statements as you learn about MASS CUSTOMIZED LEARNING.

We recommend that you come back to this section after you have read *Inevitable: Mass Customized Learning* and do the scoring again. We expect that scores will increase significantly after you have been introduced to the **MCL** vision and have had time to reflect on its potential for "leapfrogging" the Industrial Age educational paradigm.

What We Do That Doesn't Make Sense Anymore

Quick Story (cjs): I just now wiki'd "Committee of Ten." Put three words in the box, my first try, and in seconds learned the why, how, and the by whom of the curriculum and instructional design of our high schools.

Today's transformational technology is unbelievable . . . well, almost unbelievable, especially to us digital immigrants. And we don't have to be told that "you ain't seen nothing yet." Which makes the point of the label for this section. The world has changed significantly since 1892, and some of the things we continue to do in schools no longer make sense.

The Committee of Ten, a group of educators mostly from colleges and universities, was asked by the National Education Association to make recommendations regarding the standardization of American high school curriculum. The year was 1892, somewhat before cars and long before computers and the internet. Their recommendations:

☑ Twelve years of education, eight years of elementary education, followed by four years of high school.

☑ Teach English, mathematics, and history or civics to every student every academic year in high school.

☑ Teach biology, chemistry, and physics respectively in ascending high school academic years.

1892 . . . no, that's not 1992, that's **1892!** Do those recommendations ring with today's school systems? Can you think of any other profession or industry that could have pulled off that record of changeless longevity?

Members of the "Committee of Ten" *were future-focused thinkers and planners*! They created an Industrial Age education system to ready America for the future . . . for the Industrial Revolution. They succeeded. Masterfully! The United States created an educational system that was the envy of the world and the "engine" that made America great.

Much/most of what we now do in public education made good sense when it was designed, implemented, and refined throughout the Industrial Age. But we are no longer living in the Industrial Age, and some things that made sense then don't make sense today. Technology and the Information Age have changed our world.

Bell Curve Expectations:

Grading on the curve, failing students, and accepting dropouts used to make sense. They don't any more!

We now know and believe that all students can learn. Some may take more time and some may have to learn in a different way, but all can learn. Further, during the Industrial Age, a student could do poorly in school or even drop out of school and still get a good paying job as a low skilled worker. Those jobs are no longer available. Learners leaving our schools today without competitive skills are not looking at a successful and meaningful future. To us (Chuck and Bea), this is a moral imperative. If THAT doesn't motivate you, then realize it is an economic imperative.

Assembly-Line Instruction:

The graded, assembly-line organizational structure of schools used to make sense. It doesn't any more!

Students learn at different rates. (Wow, what an enlightened statement!) This fact is so universally agreed upon by everyone who has more than one child or who has taught children that it shouldn't have to be mentioned. But reality is that we continue to organize our schools as though every ten-year old is ready to learn the same thing and that every fourteen-year old is ready for Algebra. Our only debate seems to be "should we start school before or after Labor Day."

> *Quick Story (cjs):* I once heard Madeline Hunter (one of our heroines), after making a passionate and effective presentation on the need to individualize learning for youngsters, be asked, "At what age do you think a student is ready to begin Kindergarten?" Dr. Hunter calmly and assuringly answered, "That's the wrong question. The question is: What is that child ready for?" What a learning that was for me. I was about 25 at the time and had never before questioned the assembly-line structure of schools.

Time the Constant, Learning the Variable:

Student seat time as the constant (everyone has 45 minutes to learn how to subtract fractions) and learning outcomes as the variable (some kids get it, some kind of get it, and some just don't get it) used to make sense. It doesn't any more!

Allowing time rather than the quality of learning to be the gatekeeper has the immediate effect of sending some learners out the door who don't quite understand the concept that was taught, but it also has a more powerful negative impact on tomorrow's lesson and all lessons thereafter. "Not quite getting it" is cumulative. Tomorrow when "we all learn to divide fractions," the "didn't quite get it" learner doesn't have the prerequisite learnings required for clearly understanding the division of fractions. The further learners get behind in a group-paced, time-driven system, the quicker and further they will continue to fall behind.

Limited Learning Opportunities:

Teaching to the average learner or to the middle of the class, knowing that the fast learners will easily learn today's lesson and sit through the class spinning their intellectual wheels, used to make sense. It doesn't any more!

We are not letting our fast runners run. If not limited by group paced instruction, a large percentage of highly motivated achievers would be motivated to go far beyond what our top quartile learners now accomplish. The Industrial Age assembly line moves only so fast . . . too fast for some, too slow for others. We have created special costly programs for those who need extra time and additional coaching, but we leave our fast runners to be controlled by the master schedule and the curriculum.

Simultaneously Teaching 25 Unique Learners:

Expecting teachers to meet the diverse learning needs of twenty-five children simultaneously used to make sense. It doesn't any more!

The policies and practices of public schools are bureaucratic. An objective analysis of the structure of public schools clearly shows that they are designed for administrative convenience. Personalizing learning begins only after a teacher is assigned a group of students . . . and a 1/25 teacher/student ratio does not make personalization and individualization of learning doable.

Averaging Grades:

Averaging grades used to make sense. (But did it ever?) Well even if it did, it doesn't any more!

If we have to provide a rationale for why this outdated practice no longer makes sense, we are in trouble. But just to be safe, we will provide a brief explanation of our position. Grades are not a valid assessment of learning. Learning, to be validated, must be demonstrated. If you can demonstrate what you have learned, then you have learned. If you can't, you're not finished yet.

> ***Quick Story (cjs):*** *I went to a very small high school, one that didn't offer trigonometry. In college I wanted to major in math and signed up for trig. At the first class meeting, the instructor asked the forty students in attendance "How many of you have not had high school trig?" Five of us raised a hand. "Sorry guys"(and I think we were all guys,) but we are going to begin on Chapter 8." I got a "D" on my first test, an "A" on my second test, and for the final, a comprehensive test that covered the complete course, I had the highest score in the class. Mind you now, the teacher was a mathematician. One might expect logic. Want to guess my final grade?*

College Prep Curriculum:

Justifying a curriculum based upon getting students "ready for more school" used to make sense. <u>It doesn't any more!</u>

Public schools are, or should be, about preparing learners for life. If life itself doesn't provide opportunities for "rigor," what does? Education for life or for more school need not be an either/or decision. Life-role based learner outcomes quite naturally also prepare learners for additional learning. Curriculum needs to be relevant to motivate, and few of our high school students of today find their curriculum relevant to life . . . not the life they are living today or the life they expect after completing school.

Agrarian School Calendar:

Expecting learning opportunities to coincide with an agrarian calendar used to make sense. <u>It doesn't any more!</u>

In fairness, we recognize that some school systems have designed school calendars that no longer assume that the older children will be expected to help with planting and harvesting, but the majority continues to have 180-185 day calendars with two to three months of summer vacation built in. The learning regression that occurs with this traditional schedule has been documented, and experienced teachers have long recognized the need to "catch them back up" come September.

Motivation and Professionalism, Then and Now

Student motivation and educator professionalism — terms that, on the surface, don't seem to be that closely related — are cause and effect when we envision MASS CUSTOMIZED LEARNING. <u>Follow closely.</u>

PROFESSIONALISM is partially defined as "acting on/applying the research base of the profession." Students are motivated and engaged when their personal learning needs are met. **MCL** makes it possible for educators to meet the personal needs of all learners. **MCL** is a big, critical, essential win-win for students and for teachers.

A phrase we frequently hear from nearly every educational stakeholder is: "Kids just aren't motivated to learn these days." That statement shouldn't surprise anyone given the reality of today's world for children and young adults. <u>Life</u> for kids is much more exciting than school! In our day, teachers had to compete with Rock Hudson and Doris Day in the movie *Pillow Talk*. In our own children's time, they had to compete with the TV and *The Mod Squad*, *All In The Family*, and *Monday Night Football*. Tough competitions but teachers could somewhat hold their own. But today teachers compete, and get compared to, My Space, Twitter, Xbox, Gameboy, Madden Football, and any topic they may want to surf on their computer. Everything they encounter is interactive, interesting, challenging, and set at their own level of proficiency. This reality makes it easier to understand the learner quote from the intro, "When we come to school, we have to power down."

MOTIVATION: What motivates people to learn? What do we know about motivation and engagement – from our most basic professional research, from our personal experiences as learners, and from our experiences as parents and teachers? Our study of students and learning, and our experience as parents and teachers, make it rather clear that learner motivation and engagement are in large part the result of:

Meeting learners at their readiness level:

Research strongly indicates that the number one determiner of learning success is the learner's "prerequisite learnings." That is, does the learner have the background knowledge and/or skills necessary to understand the new concept, process, or skill being taught? For example, if you are teaching a youngster to multiply 84 times 36, the chances of her learning it is very dependent upon her already being able to add and knowing her timetables.

Accommodating personal learning styles:

There are many ways of being intelligent and many modes of learning. We all tend to be better at some learning modes than others. Some learn easily or best when reading, some when listening, some when watching, some when interacting with others, some learn best when doing it, when simply struggling through it. So, when a teacher uses one basic mode of teaching, it is working for some learners and not for others.

Learning through content that is personally interesting:

To learn new concepts, ideas, opinions, etc. we typically interact with existing information and/or data. For example, we can learn about the concept of "racism" by studying the Civil War, the life and teachings of Martin Luther King, how Jackie Robinson broke the Major League Baseball color barrier, today's life on a Native American reservation, or many other arenas of "content" that would be exciting to some and boring to others.

MASS CUSTOMIZED LEARNING, as described and explained in the remainder of _Inevitable_, makes it possible to consistently apply each of these three intrinsic motivators to student learning. Without intrinsic motivation engaging the learner, educators must apply extrinsic motivation, and frequently that motivation takes the form of manipulation, coercion, and grades as punishment and reward. Today's predominant assembly line organizational structure makes it impossible to simultaneously apply these three basic motivators to 25 students.

So there you have it, the win-win, the cause and effect of professionalism — applying our best research to intrinsically motivate learners, which when done . . . intrinsically motivates learners.

Our best teachers are attempting to do this now in a structure that is not designed to encourage or support it. What might these teachers accomplish if their beliefs about individualizing learning were openly and intentionally encouraged and supported by the organization's structure? Well, we would have professionals helping intrinsically motivated, engaged learners to achieve faster and further than ever before.

Individualizing Instruction, a Brief Historical Perspective

Reflective, learner-centered teachers who have ever taught in a public school have dreamt about being able to individualize and personalize learning for students. They knew intuitively that children learned on different days and in different ways. We (Chuck and Bea) go back a long way, and we have been dreaming for a long time.

In 1965, President Johnson signed a sweeping bill we came to refer to as "The Elementary and Secondary Education Act of l965," and with that bill, the federal government became involved in public education.

The bill contained a number of programs, the most noted and most lasting was/is labeled Title I. Title I focused on the learning needs of children of low income families. Title III of the bill had to do with innovation and change. Even our legislators knew then that education needed to change significantly if it were to meet the needs of learners and the needs of our society. Title III, for future-focused educators, was the exciting part of that legislation. Most of the Title III efforts had to do with some form of "Individualizing Instruction." But this was the Industrial Age, and the assembly line approach to instruction was accepted as a given. (Come to think about it, we have whipped right past the Information Age and the educational assembly line is still accepted as a given.)

Dr. Madeline Hunter, Principal of the UCLA lab school, was probably the most respected consultant of the day. She was deep in research, had an enviable track record, and was a great presenter . . . as well as a great person. She and Dr. John Goodlad, also of UCLA, and Dr. Dwight Allen, Professor at Stanford and later Dean of the School of Education at the University of Massachusetts, were the innovative thinkers of the day . . . and they all promoted "Individualized Instruction." Their strategies took the form of team teaching, non-graded schools, multi-age grouping, flexible scheduling, etc. All these strategies were still basically within the assembly line structure.

The point here is that educational professionals have known what needs to be done for a long time, but we were stuck in a "group paced" paradigm that we couldn't escape. In all fairness, we did not have the tools to escape that paradigm. But now we do. Madeline should be with us today. She would quickly recognize the opportunity. Chapter 2, "The Future IS Now: Transformational Technologies," begins to frame MASS CUSTOMIZED LEARNING, our vision of how educators can use today's tools to personalize and individualize learning for all students every day.

A closing note: To help you to recognize false prophets, even the moral, true believer, passionate type false prophets, you must apply this test. If the innovation/change they are promoting retains the bureaucratic assembly line delivery of instruction, they are not talking about transforming education. They are talking about "tinkering" with an old outdated paradigm in hopes of "catching up" with Singapore, South Korea, and Catholic Schools. **MCL** is about "leapfrogging," not about catching up with those who are the most efficient at being obsolete.

Chapter 1
Takeaways:

Educators, and especially educational leaders, must get in touch with, articulate, and accept today's harsh realities if we are to have a platform from which to create transformational change.

Much of what we now do made sense when we were living and learning in the Industrial Age. We are no longer living in the Industrial Age and much of what we continue to do no longer makes sense.

Intrinsically motivating today's learners and applying professional practices are closely related. You can't have one without the other. Professional practices, in the form of applying our most basic research, is the "cause;" high achieving, intrinsically motivated learners is the "effect." Win-Win is the outcome.

"Denial is not a river that runs through Egypt."

Pam Tillis, C&W Artist

The Future Is Now: Transformational Technologies

"I used to think that cyberspace was fifty years away.
What I thought was fifty years away, was only ten years away.
And what I thought was ten years away...it was already here.
I just wasn't aware of it yet."

Bruce Sterling

"Perhaps it's time to retire Santayana's old canard:
'Those who do not learn from history are bound to repeat it.'
And replace it with:
'Those who cannot anticipate and prepare for the future
will suffer in it.'"

William Gibson

Chapter 2 Intent

To show/convince educators that the technology required to customize learning for each learner is available NOW and has already proven itself to be effective and efficient.

Some of the new whiz-bang technologies make us faster at doing what we have always done. And that's good. Handheld calculators made us much faster at dividing three digit numbers. Microwaves made us faster at warming up leftovers. But we still divide three digit numbers and we still warm up leftovers.

And then there are whiz-whiz-bang-bang technologies that go even further — they transform "how" we do things. Smartphones "transformed" how we communicate and keep track of our world. It's almost a bit sad to walk through an airport today and see those pay phones with no customers. Amazon. com, with the advent of the Kindle 2, might just have made books obsolete. Do we still call someone's extended essays that are downloaded to our electronic reader a "book?" Should I be unloading my Barnes & Noble stock?

Transformational technologies are disruptive. They have the power to make traditional tools and processes obsolete virtually overnight. It seems like just yesterday that we were buying film, taking pictures, having photos developed, and really quite pleased with the process and the results. When the first digital camera hit the market, a whole industry was doomed. And you didn't have to be a "futurist" to recognize it. We had moved from film to digits, from photo albums to slide shows, and from professional photographers to computer programs that "enhance" our somewhat amateur shots and ready them for distribution.

Transformational technologies are disruptive. They have the power to make traditional tools and processes obsolete virtually overnight.

We (Chuck and Bea) are not futurists. We are "trend-trackers." There is a big difference between the two. Futurists rely on insights and do a lot of guessing. Sometimes they are right. Trend-trackers keep their eyes on the horizon so they can be one of the first to see what's coming. They are much more likely to be accurate. And they should be because, for them, the future IS now. They see the trend before they label it and before they point it out to others.

Mass Customization, made possible by today's transformational technologies, is the strong and disruptive trend with the power to transform education. Customizing, individualizing, and personalizing education to meet the learning needs of every learner is inevitable! Educators have long dreamed about individualizing and personalizing education for all learners. Now they have the tools to make their dreams and visions come true.

Mass Customization

"Mass Customizing" is a bit hard to define, but quite easily understood. Before the onslaught of today's transformational technologies, "mass customization" could have been seen as an oxymoron. "Mass" and "customizing" just didn't go together. Rather like "jumbo shrimp." When living in the Industrial Age, we were the happy recipients of this great new technology labeled "mass production." We all got the same products, there were enough to go around and, if not, we would simply restart the assembly line and make some more. Think Ford cars, Zenith televisions, Scott Foresman basal readers.

But somewhere in the past five to seven years we started to see the term "mass customization" everywhere in leadership and change literature. Today's technology now allows us to not only make as many as the people want, but also to make them exactly the size and color we want. Think iPods, HP computers, Starbucks, My Yahoo home page.

> *In short, Mass Production is to the Industrial Age as Mass Customization is to the Information Age.*

Even in the Industrial Age we could get products and services customized if we were willing to pay the price. We could have our kitchen cabinets custom made to fit our kitchen floor plan and our discriminating tastes, but we expected them to cost more than those ready made and sold at the lumberyard. The unmaking of the "mass customization" oxymoron happened when we could not only customize products and services, but when we could also customize at the same cost that we used to pay for those "mass produced." With that intro, we come to our definition of Mass Customization.

> # Mass Customization:
>
> *the capacity to routinely customize products and services*
> *to meet the specific needs and/or desires of individuals*
> *without adding significantly to the cost of the product or service.*

Mass customization has snuck up on many of us. It has happened gradually and has moved from industry to industry without carrying the "mass customizing" label. We have gotten used to having our products and services customized without having the label "mass customizing" used to define what is happening. We take mass customization for granted. We turn on our computer, click on "Word," choose our favorite font, our color of the day, and the stationery that we think will impress our reader, and within seconds we are creating a document that we have quickly and effortlessly customized to meet our personal desires.

Cross-Industry Learning

But let's stop here for a moment. What are your thoughts as you experience mass customization nearly everywhere you go . . . well maybe except for stoplights? Do you think, "Gee, that was easy and it's exactly what I wanted," and go on your way. Or do you think, "Gee, this is really something . . . getting exactly what I wanted while others are also getting exactly what they wanted . . . and, for a good price." You ask...

☑ "How do they do that?"

Now if you asked yourself that question, and when you learned the answer, asked yourself a second question,

☑ "How could I apply this method of mass customization to education, to my school, to my classroom?"

You have now set yourself up as a "cross-industry learner." And those two questions take you to where we want you to go with this chapter. (More about cross-industry learning later.)

Chuck's Mass Customized Day

We were tempted to take editing liberties as we thought of this section; tempted to have a good time by making a typical day seem a bit James Bondish. But again, in the spirit of transparency, we have instead chosen to describe a day in Joe Friday fashion . . . you do remember Dragnet . . . "just the facts, Ma'am." Chuck, in his own words:

A bit of context might help as you follow me through Thursday, March 24, 2010. I am a 70-year old male and have been an educator all of my adult life. Although I don't feel retired, I live in a retirement community in the Phoenix area during the winter months. I have been a serious student and teacher of leadership, change, and future conditions for forty years. I don't know much about how technology works, but I can work it. I have a good grasp about the power of today's technology, and especially about its power and potential to transform education.

6 a.m.: I am off to the Rec. Center and the exercise room. I set (customize) my treadmill at a speed of 4.0 with an incline of 10 degrees. Turn on my iPod and listen to (customized) music that makes your pants want to get up and dance. The treadmill dashboard tells me how long I have been on the machine, the number of calories I have burned, and my heart rate. I change settings so that I finish my cardiovascular exercise of the day having burned 350 calories . . . the exact amount that will allow me to eat a Snickers candy bar this afternoon without feeling guilty.

The exercise room has machines that can test every muscle in your body . . . well, almost every muscle. Each machine has at least three settings that allow the user to "customize" his / her workout. After 25 minutes of that, I tell myself that I have earned a trip to Starbucks.

7 a.m.: *Starbucks and a (customized) venti half-caf for me and a venti chai, no fat, no foam, no water, and 8 pumps for Genny, my bride of 50 years. It is a busy place, the line moves fast, we hardly ever wait more than two minutes for our (customized) drinks.*

This is our quiet time for reading. We look for the most comfortable place to sit and spend 45 minutes reading and sometimes sharing the exciting things we are learning. We each have a Kindle 2 reader that allows us to (customize) download our choice of books from anywhere in less than a minute. We choose our book, our font size, and Starbucks' softest chairs. Everyone who passes by seems to want to know how we like those Kindles.

8 a.m.: *Am at home and I just talked with the Engelhardts who want to visit us this weekend and play some golf. I need a Saturday tee time. With one click on my bookmark Golf Now (a customized service, of course), I can find available tee times and special deals for more than 100 Phoenix area courses. I select the course (there is a good deal at the Union Hills Country Club) and click "purchase." One click is all it takes because they have my Visa card number. I am informed that I will have to wear a shirt with a collar and will have to wear my cap with the bill forward. How did they know I was from South Dakota?*

9 a.m.: *Time to catch up on today's news. I get five daily papers . . . well, I don't really get five papers, but I do have five on my Bookmark list. My sources range from the conservative Wall Street Journal to the liberal New York Times.*

I don't get the ads or the classifieds, I don't pay anything for subscriptions, I don't cause trees to be felled, nor trucks to transport. And, of course, no need to recycle digits. But my favorite news source is My Yahoo Home Page, which I have been able to design (ah, make that "customize") according to my interests, tastes, values, and biases. I have the only My Yahoo Home Page of its kind.

10 a.m. or so: *My friends and family meet almost daily on Facebook. I get to select my friends and family, and sometimes a family member actually fits into both categories! Genny and I are both from families of ten and at one count, years ago, we had 122 nieces and nephews. We don't send Christmas gifts. Facebook has given us the opportunity to rekindle and deepen our important relationships. We all get to choose (customize) how we portray ourselves, what information we choose to share, which photos we think will be of interest, and who will have access to our posts. We are in charge; we get to "customize" our Facebook communications.*

11 a.m. *or whenever I feel that I have procrastinated long enough . . . then there is work, or whatever you may choose to call the writing I am doing right now. Like many "free agents" today, I can choose when I work, where I work, how I work, and for whom I work. I can "customize" my day to fit my work goals and my desired lifestyle. Starbucks is my meeting room, Kinkos is my print shop, my iPhone / iPad is my office manager, my email system has replaced the post office, and my computer has become my secretary.*

We could go on with the remainder of the day, but we are quite sure that you have gotten the message. The activities described above are real and they are quite typical. There is little doubt that they will become even more the norm in the future.

Technology has helped us to move our world from mass production to mass customization . . . with the striking exception of our public school systems and the education of our youth. Here, where customized learning could/should have its most positive impact, school systems and educators continue to apply seriously outdated and bureaucratic Industrial Age policies, practices, and structures. Our assembly line instructional delivery system, where we teach as though "one size fits all," couldn't be more out of step with what we know about students and learning. MASS CUSTOMIZED LEARNING is right, it is available, and it is <u>inevitable</u>.

The Larger Picture and Influence of Transformational Technology

To further define and clarify the power transformational technology and mass customization are having on our society, we share the following **From—To** listing:

From THE INDUSTRIAL AGE	To THE INFORMATION AGE
from.... The Organization	to....The Customer / Client
from.... Them in Control	to.... I'm in Charge
from.... One Way Communication	to.... Two Way Dialogue
from.... Broadcasting	to.... Blogging
from.... They Create	to.... I Design
from.... Their Judgments	to.... My Needs / Desires
from.... Their Values & Biases	to.... My Values & Biases
from.... Unwanted Commercials	to.... Customer Reviews
from.... You Need Me	to.... Excuse Me!

These subtle, and sometimes not so subtle, shifts have moved the locus of power from the business to the customer, from the organization to the individual, and from formal leadership to groups and social networks. Individuals and informal groups are feeling their power. They are feeling and acting as though they are empowered. Try this on: Bill Spady, an insightful friend and colleague, believes that "we are living in the Age of Empowerment." We agree.

Who Is Doing It Now: Cross-Industry Learning

A basic premise of this chapter, and this book, is that the technology to mass customize education already exists and is being used effectively in a variety of professions and industries today. Educators need only to apply cross-industry learning techniques to enable themselves to apply mass customizing techniques and strategies to education. Stop for a moment to think of what would happen to student motivation if:

. . . *every day, every learner came to school and was met with (customized) learning activities at his/her precise developmental and achievement level, was learning in one of his/her most effective learning modes, was learning with content of interest to himself/herself, was challenged, was successful, and left school eager to come back tomorrow.*

It could be! Later, in Chapter 7, we will be more specific about what it could look like and how to do it. But for now we would like to take you on a tour of effective companies and industries that are doing for their customers and clients what we need to do for learners if the above vision is to be realized. And it will be realized; it's, well......inevitable.

Apple, Inc.

Just a few years ago we thought that the CD was the end-all technology for the music industry. But that was when the music industry was in charge. Today, the customer, the listener, is in charge. Apple has mass customized the selection process, the delivery process, and the listening experience . . . and is doing it cheaper than ever before . . . all while making big dollars and seeing their stock prices soar.

Many of us have had the experience of downloading a favorite song of the day from a library of more than six million songs. iTunes makes it easy to find that song and download it directly to your iPhone in about a minute. All with one click. Your Visa card is debited, the artist's account is credited, and you are one-half of a duo doing "I Did It My Way" with Frank Sinatra. All friction free. No one did any work, no one other than you touched anything. And Steve Jobs buys another bottle of expensive Merlot.

Now what would a "cross-industry learner" do with that experience? Well, they would go beyond "Gee, what will they think of next!" Now what were those two enabling questions:

1) How does Apple/iTunes do that? . . . . .and
2) How might we educators use this technology to meet the needs and desires of <u>our</u> customers – our students, our learners?

An example might be helpful here.

First question: "How does Apple do that?"

Well, I don't know the "tech geek" explanation, but I do understand that there is a technology that allows customers to quickly find what they want from an inventory of virtually every song that has ever been recorded; to quickly download things of interest to his/her personal computer; to facilitate, record, and make available the transaction specifics to anyone with a need-to-know.

Second question: "What are the implications of this technology for education?"

Gee, what if we could put all of our learner outcomes in a library much like Apple does music; make our outcomes, with accompanying technology-driven learning opportunities available to those learners who need that learning experience right now, 24/7; and, record that whole experience and demonstration of learning in a personalized electronic portfolio for review by the student, parents, teachers, leaders, and the school system's records department.

Amazon.com

Apple and Amazon may be the two most obvious examples of applying transformational technology to change the game . . . not just the strategies, but THE GAME. Amazon.com leapfrogged the book industry by selling books online, they now may be in the process of making "books" obsolete with their Kindle electronic reader, and to top it all off, they are not even in the book sales business. They are in the "electronic retail sales" business and have become the largest and most respected e-retailer on the net. They sell boots as well as books. Amazon's core competencies are about profiling, about linking producers with buyers, about customer evaluations of products, and about electronic money exchange. They can plug any product into their system, run it through their process, and exit with satisfied customers.

So, what might an educator who is a cross-industry learner take away from the Amazon.com experience? Our first thought is about profiling, a word that is not usually considered politically correct but, in this case, is a good thing. How does Amazon know what books will be of interest to me? Obviously they know the authors I read and the subject matter of the books I have purchased. And if I want to cooperate with them in their attempt to sell me things, I can voluntarily submit info about my interests. Mr. Amazon is happy to hear from me.

But, look one level deeper and you will find that Amazon "tags" me (Chuck), the books I buy, and every book they sell. Google and Bing do the same type of "tagging" with everything on their search sites. iTunes does it with songs and artists that they then use to put that "genius" list on the right side of your screen . . . as if by magic, they know that if you like Waylon Jennings, chances are quite good that you will also like Merle Haggard. And chances are that you might like to buy that Haggard tune for only 99 cents, which you can do with one click, of course. (Note: If you want a good read to understand "tagging," read _Everything Is Miscellaneous_ by Weinberger. One of the best books we have read to help us understand technology at one level below the magic that you see on your computer screen.)

Well that sort of answers the "how do they do that" question. So let's move to the cross-industry learning question, "How might that technology be applied to education?" Amazon knows me. They know my name, my purchasing history, my preferences . . . like, they know I buy only non-fiction books . . . I am attracted by books about leadership, change, and the future. It doesn't take much for Mr. Amazon to know that I might be interested in a new book titled _The 100 Best Business Books of All Time_ by Covert and Sattersten.

All they needed was the whiz-bang technology to put Schwahn, my past book purchases, and the title of the new book together and, like magic, when I next open my Amazon account, there is the book I obviously need to have. Coincidentally, it's the very book that I had been attracted to when recently browsing at Barnes and Noble. Amazon can do that because 1) "Schwahn," 2) the content of the past books Schwahn has purchased, and 3) the new title _The 100 Best Business Books of All Time_ all have been given a "leadership" tag.

(A fun but true fact: the guys down at Jiffy Lube know my 1990 F150 pickup better than my doctor knows my blood pressure condition. All Mr. Jiffy needs is my license number and they are ready with my history and their recommendations. They even know that six months ago I didn't buy that air cleaner they suggested.)

Might Amazon's profiling competencies be used to help us identify the best/ most effective learning styles of individual learners? Might their profiling insights and skills be used to identify the topics, content, people, or activities that interest that outgoing fifth grade girl or that quiet 15-year old boy who always finds a seat in the back row? The right or best learning style, along with content that is of high interest to the learner, are two of the most powerful motivators in the learning game. Hit these two buttons and apply the right level of difficulty to the learner outcome at hand, and you have a motivated, self-starting learner.

We went into some detail with the Apple and Amazon examples above and expect that we can now be a bit briefer as we identify other businesses/organizations that are using technology to transform their profession, business, or industry. In other words, we expect that you "got" the two questions pondered by the cross-industry learner.

Verizon

Amazing how you can get your monthly bill from Verizon or AT&T and find that they have routinely listed every call you made, the numbers that you called, the date and time of your call, how many minutes you spoke, and seldom make an error. No errors in my seven years with a cell phone. And truth be known, they could probably tell you the topic of your conversations if privacy laws allowed it. (Just a thought, but with the video capacity of our new smartphones, they might also be able to tell you what you were wearing when you made the call. Careful there!)

Might Verizon have already created a system that would allow a similar record of each student's accomplishments in real time? A record that could be available to "anyone with a need to know" 24/7? Rather than the phone call info listed in the example above, the record might include learner outcomes that have been accomplished, a link to an electronic portfolio that shows the student's demonstration of that outcome, and a listing of "next" learner outcomes for your son or daughter. Maybe even a link to dinner conversation topics or other activities that would help the learner to more fully understand the topic.

Wells Fargo

Remember when banks were open from 9 to 3 for your inconvenience? Now we have access 24/7/52. (Is that how we cleverly say "all the time?") What might Wells Fargo teach us about how we could make it convenient for "anyone to learn anything from anywhere at any time from worldwide experts?"

Google/Bing

Google and Bing can get any information you want in three clicks or less. Google and Bing have become verbs . . . as in "Just a second, I'll Google that." (Well, not quite anything I guess; they don't seem to be able to tell me where I left those leather gloves that I paid big bucks for!)

What might we learn from Google and Bing that will help us to put our complete curriculum and accompanying learning strategies online to be accessed by anyone from anywhere at any time? Why not just put our curriculum on Google or Bing? Of course, this assumes that your curriculum, your learner outcomes, and the accompanying learning activities for those things that are best learned with a computer have been created. So get at it! We'll tell you how later.

Facebook

Facebook, conceptualized by a college student as a system/program for linking college students on a single campus with friends enrolled in common classes to share ideas and study together, has grown to become the leading social network of the day. Both McGarvey and Schwahn are Facebook enthusiasts. We have our listing of friends, and then we have a subgroup of family friends. It is a great way to keep in touch, to share anything from earth shattering news to trivia, to share photos, videos, and anything you might have found interesting on YouTube that you think might also be found interesting by friends or family. Great for dialogue, discussion, or chit-chat.

For us, Facebook seems like an ideal way to link learners and learning facilitators together in their study of concepts/learner outcomes that require shared information, dialogue, and give-and-take in a seminar format. Not all about teacher to students, but also about learner-to-learner, and learner to learning facilitator. (More about seminars and their place in **MCL** in Chapter 7.)

Wikipedia

We have talked some . . . and will continue to talk . . . about the potential of mass customization, but there is another "mass" out there that also has powerful implications for education and learning. The label is "mass collaboration," and the poster child for that concept is Wikipedia.

As we mentioned earlier, transformational technology is disruptive technology. It's a game changer. It often puts good "old reliables" out of business. Remember when encyclopedias were sold by door-to-door salesmen and Britannica was king? Buy a set and be assured that your seventh grader would be able to do those required essays and reports, get good grades, and go to college. And for just a few dollars more, you could get the one book every few years that would update the series. . . and in ten years or so, you could buy a totally new edition. Convenient payment plan available.

> *As we mentioned earlier, transformational technology is disruptive technology. It's a game changer. It often puts good "old reliables" out of business.*

We won't retell the Wikipedia story or describe the process of creation as we expect that you already know their story. But know that Wikipedia was created by volunteers and is continually updated by volunteers willing to give their time to something of interest and importance. The Linux operating system is another example of mass collaboration. A very good read to understand and learn how to harness the mass collaboration process and power is Clay Shirky's *Here Comes Everybody*.

Implications for education and learning: 1) Wikipedia, along with Google, can make many of today's textbooks unnecessary. Save the textbook money and spend it on laptops for everyone. Teachers and students alike can find nearly any concept/idea/event they have ever thought of defined, described, and explained. 2) How about using the mass collaboration technology that has been so successful for Wikipedia to allow and motivate educators to create alternative curricula, learner outcomes, and associated learning strategies? Far from being a national curriculum, this process could create alternatives that could save the reinvention of the wheel and hasten our profession's move toward MASS CUSTOMIZED LEARNING.

Yahoo Calendar

If you haven't caught the central message yet, know that we are well aware that education cannot be significantly improved if we continue to rely on the assembly line, time-driven instructional delivery system that doesn't take learner needs and learner variability into consideration. If we discard the administratively convenient assembly line, we will need to replace it with a flexible scheduling system that focuses on the learner; a system that makes learning the constant and time the variable rather than our present structure that does the opposite . . . that makes time the constant and quality learning the variable. Yahoo, Microsoft, Google, and many other businesses offer electronic calendars with the power to schedule highly complex personal agendas.

Walmart

Yes, Walmart! What Walmart has done with the barcode is near genius. With one scan of a product barcode, Walmart can tell you more than you want to know about that electric toothbrush that you are looking at in the health section. Its cost, their inventory, their supplier, date of next shipment, etc. etc. A humanized application of the Walmart system could allow school leaders to be anywhere and still be accountable for the whereabouts of each student, for the real-time accessing of individual student learning activities, for emergency medical information, etc. etc.

It is interesting to note that Walmart customizes its shopping not with mass customizing technology, but with inventory. They just make their stores large enough to have an "everything" inventory. "If you can't find it at Walmart, God didn't want you to have it."

Education, a Business

Well yes, education is a business. It is probably the largest business in your community when all is considered, and easily the most important. It is also an industry badly in need of becoming a profession. But above all of that, education is an organization; an organization with a constituency that needs and deserves the most up-to-date tools and strategies. The school system IS the most important organization in your community.

We hope and trust that applying effective business practices isn't a mind closer for you. All successful businesses seek cross-industry learning opportunities. We are ripe for that type of openness. Cross-industry learning provides educators an opportunity to not only catch up with those best at applying Industrial Age structures and practices, but to leapfrog them much like Apple and Amazon. com have leapfrogged their old paradigm competitors.

It is our strong opinion that MASS CUSTOMIZED LEARNING has the power to move public education from a bureaucratic industry to an effective and efficient profession. Teachers should and would embrace that opportunity. You will see as we continue our explanation of **MCL** that being a professional requires that we apply our best and most basic research. Our present assembly line organizational structure doesn't encourage, nor allow, teachers to act on individual learning needs, respond to individual learning styles, or to teach a concept or a skill using content of interest to the learner. Until we are able to meet learners at their personal need level in these three basic categories, it will be difficult to think of our work as a profession.

Closing Notes for Chapter 2

Note 1:
In this chapter, we presented several opportunities that educators have for cross-industry learning. We hope that you found them all interesting, understandable, and relevant. We would also expect that you have a big question that might approximate this . . . "Yeah, Schwahn and McGarvey, all of these examples you give are interesting and relevant, but what would our school systems actually look like if we were doing all of those things? How does all of this fit together? Remember, we have to actually run a school and manage a classroom. It gets real when you have to apply these ideas with real teachers and real students. We don't have the luxury to just sit around and philosophize; we live in the real world."

Well, maybe we just got carried away and you didn't say that much, but in any case, hang tight; before you finish *Inevitable*, we will put it all together for you in an exciting yet logical manner, and you will see **MCL** to be desirable, exciting, professional, and doable.

Note 2:
We realize that it is difficult . . . make that very difficult for educators and parents to think and act outside of the box (OTB) when it comes to education. We have all been in school for a good portion of our lives, some of us for all of our adult lives, and "we have always done it that way."

- *Our laws have legalized our assembly line, time-driven schools,*
- *Parents have internalized that outdated paradigm,*
- *Educators have institutionalized that way of doing things, and*
- *Our media continues to support back-to-the-future type change.*

It is almost unbelievable to Schwahn and McGarvey that our most highly regarded transformational thinkers can create the iPhone, operationalize mass collaboration efforts, and upset the entire book publishing business, but when it comes to educational change, they all become tinkerers. They try to improve the old paradigm of schooling. Even they don't seem to be able to think OTB when it comes to schools and school systems. So yes, we know OTB thinking is always difficult and doubly so for teachers, parents, and school leaders. And that's probably why our schools have existed for more than a century essentially as is, without meaningful change.

But stay with us. Don't despair. **MCL** is a logical and rational way to significantly change education. We wouldn't be so positive about that if we didn't see the proven transformational technologies all around us, just waiting to be applied to learning, learners, and learning systems. Trust us.

Chapter 2
Takeaways:

We live in a world that is mass customizing nearly all products and services. Power has shifted from the producer to the customer and the customer has been empowered to expect and accept only those things that meet his/her specific needs and desires.

Proven technology with the capacity to effectively and efficiently implement MASS CUSTOMIZED LEARNING is routinely being used in businesses and industries today.

Educators must embrace "cross-industry learning" if education and educators are to join the mass customized, customer-centered world of business and effective organizations.

Chapter 3

But First....Our Purpose

"What business are we in?
The answer seemed obvious . . . and that was the problem."

Theodore Levitt

"The question matters because
the corporation (school system) holds
some assumptions so deeply that they disappear from view."

"It is the job of the leader to ferret out these assumptions
and release the organization from them."

Grant McCracken

Chapter 3 Intent

To convince you that the purpose of education is to prepare students to live successful and meaningful lives . . . and that doing so also prepares students for more school should they choose. We also plan to show you how to create a compelling organizational purpose.

As we begin to think about the purpose of schooling, it would be good to study the following definitions with the title of Chapter 3, "*But First . . . Our Purpose*" in mind.

As regards our most basic purpose(s), what are we doing that is largely based on habit and tradition? Is what we are now doing logical or illogical? Do we even give "purpose" much thought? If we were to make the purpose of our school system clear and logical, what would it take? What questions would we be asking ourselves in order to encourage and ensure "clear sound reasoning?"

<u>Habit</u>: *a settled or regular tendency or practice*
<u>Tradition</u>: *the transmission of customs from generation to generation*
<u>Illogical</u>: *lacking sense or clear, sound reasoning*
<u>Logical</u>: *of or according to the rules of logic, characterized by clear sound reasoning*

A Little Story (cjs): I remember well my days as a twenty-five year old first-year principal preparing to open the new Laura Ingalls Wilder Elementary School that just happened to be located in **the** *Little Town on the Prairie, De Smet, South Dakota. Laura is big in this little town. I had just completed my Masters degree, had a State Department-issued administrative certificate, and two weeks to prepare for the opening of school.*

Panic!! What does a principal do to get ready for the school year? "Preparing for Opening Day" was not one of the dozen classes I had taken and, in fact, was never even a discussion topic as I negotiated thirty-three hours of credit and a thesis paper on my way to becoming "credentialed." Even before "Who Wants To Be A Millionaire?" I knew that I needed a "lifeline." Phil Vik had been my principal in my only teaching job and he was good, he was organized, he was a good manager, he knew how to run a school.

So I called Phil. And he was good. He pulled out his last year's agenda for opening day, took me through it item by item . . . introductions, the school calendar, the master schedule including recess times, P.E., Music, Art, etc., where and when to pick up your textbooks, expectations for classroom control, the schedule for selling tickets to HS sporting events, noon duty, and so on. We won't go any further with this agenda as we expect that you have been there and done that.

Well, that was yesterday. That was 1964. Enjoyable to reminisce a bit. But when thinking of how Laura Ingalls Wilder will open this year, we expect that not much has changed. The principals since my tenure might even have found that opening of school folder that I left in the file. And they very likely get ready to "have school" or to "do school" much like I did. Much like children do when they play school, where it is about directions and control, and has little to do with direction, focus and purpose.

The Purpose of Schools

No one in '64 asked or discussed the purpose of education. The purpose was obvious, it was evident, it was to "have school." And sadly, not much has changed. Now we still "have school," but we **are more focused,** we now have school so that our students will pass the state standards tests.

Very few school systems have systematically studied the learner, the future conditions awaiting graduates, the knowledge and skills needed to meet life's future challenges and opportunities, and then systematically created a curriculum and instructional system designed to ensure that students leave with that requisite knowledge and those requisite skills and attitudes. And even fewer school systems follow through when such planning has been done.

In reality, we still "have school:"

☑ Textbooks **are** our curriculum,

☑ The assembly line **is** our delivery system, and

☑ Passing tests **is** our purpose

At this point it might be helpful to look again at the preceding definitions. Educators do what they do regarding purpose and direction out of _habit and tradition_. We have done it this way (having another year of school) for as long as any of us can remember. And, for years and years it worked quite well. Schools served the needs of society and the needs of our economic system. Those who were "college material" went to college; those educated in the same system but not "college material" would find Industrial Age type jobs, make a living, raise a family, and maybe even send their children to college. The numbers and ratios of "college material" and "not college material" seemed to fit quite well.

Leadership, the Short Version

"Having School" or "Doing School" required good management and therefore efficient managers. In the Industrial Age, leadership and management were thought to be synonymous. Peter Drucker, the father of the study of management, to his dying day refused to differentiate between the two terms. But today, and maybe first initiated by the publication in 1983 of Peters and Waterman's _In Search of Excellence,_ leadership stands for more, much more, than efficient management. Effective and successful leaders, in addition to being efficient managers, are clear about the purpose, the mission, and the focus of the organization they lead.

Chapter 10, entitled "_Total Leaders,_" is a rather detailed description of the role of the leader in the creation of a MASS CUSTOMIZED LEARNING Community, but we think that it will help you, the reader, to understand the chapters between here and there if we identify the five Leadership Domains and the five Pillars of Change of the Total Leader (See Schwahn and Spady's _Total Leaders 2.0_, 2010). You will quickly note that "purpose" finds its way into the first Leadership Domain.

Total Leaders, based on the work of 50+ leading leadership gurus, are:

Leadership Domain	Major Performance Role of the Domain	Pillar of Change
Authentic Leaders *who help their organization to*	*Create a Compelling Organization Purpose*	*.... and thereby Create the Reason to Change*
Visionary Leaders *who*	*Concretely Describe the Organization's Vision*	*.... and thereby Create the Picture of the Change*
Relational Leaders *who*	*Involve Everyone in the Change Process*	*.... and thereby Create the Commitment to the Change*
Quality Leaders *who*	*Develop and Empower Everyone*	*.... and thereby Create the Capacity to Change*
Service Leaders *who*	*Manage the Vision*	*.... and thereby Create the Support for the Change*

All five Leadership Domains are critical to transformational change. If you don't do them all, you don't get the MASS CUSTOMIZED LEARNING. But, for this chapter, we focus on the first domain: *Authentic Leaders Creating a Compelling Organizational Purpose.*

You may wish to earmark this page and refer to it off and on throughout the rest of the book. (We promise to tell your librarian, and your mother, that you had our written permission to "earmark" this otherwise perfectly good book.)

Asking Yourself the "Logical" Questions

Please refer to the definitions at the beginning of this chapter. We will be asking ourselves questions that force us from the illogical to the logical, from "winging it" to clearly and systematically determining the purpose of our school system. We will move from habit and tradition as our direction-setting decision screen, to a reality, research, future conditions, and learner need-based decision screen. We will move from management to leadership. We will move from the assembly line to mass customized learning. We will exit the Industrial Age and pick up the transformational technology of the Information Age as we speed toward MASS CUSTOMIZED LEARNING and the Age of Empowerment.

Ten Critical Strategic Design Questions

Schwahn Leadership Associates has helped more than forty school systems create a Strategic Design for their organization. Some time ago we decided to call our process Strategic Design rather than Strategic Planning to differentiate our process from those done on the back of a napkin or those created in four hours at the Board's annual retreat.

We believe strongly that a plan is not "strategic" and shouldn't be called strategic unless it is:

☑ Learner Centered,

☑ Future Focused, and

☑ Based on the Best Research Regarding Students and Learning

We know of no other strategic planning process that is true to these three criteria. Further, we believe that meaningful change is only probable when all stakeholder groups are meaningfully involved in the process. We typically work with a group of 80 to 120 people representing students, teachers, parents, school leaders, board members, the business community, political leaders, law enforcement, and the clergy.

Our work schedule is flexible to fit the needs of the system, but typically we work for about 16 to 18 hours over a three-day period. We have never failed to reach group consensus on a Strategic Direction for a school system. We believe that this success is due in large part to the logical nature of the process, the questions that are asked and answered by the group, and the meaningful involvement of the total community. People leave the Strategic Design planning process believing they were heard, that they had influence, and being proud of the work they have done. They leave as community advocates for the new direction and the new vision.

Note: *Strategic Design cannot begin with a needs assessment if we want to create an Information Age, learner empowerment vision for our school system. Our present Industrial Age schools are* IN-THE-BOX. *If we start by studying how we can improve an obsolete structure, we will continue to think of how we can improve the components of an outdated, underperforming system. We can only get* OUT-OF-THE-BOX *if we ask ourselves the right questions: questions that allow us to think freely, creatively, and logically. Anything we do to try to improve our assembly line schools will be "tinkering" at best, when what is needed is a future-focused transformational vision. We don't want to catch up with those who are the best at being obsolete; we need to leapfrog them!*

Please read through and reflect upon the following ten questions so that you might get a global sense of what the Strategic Design process values and how we analyze the direction setting process. We will then provide a short narrative that will further define each question and describe in part how we facilitate the group decision making process.

1. *Do school systems exist to get students ready for life or to get ready for more school?*
2. *In what arenas do successful adults live their lives, what are the basic spheres of living?*
3. *What are the future conditions in each of the arenas / spheres of living, what will life be like, what will be the challenges and opportunities?*
4. *Given these future conditions in this (each) sphere of living, what will our graduates have to <u>know</u>, be able to <u>do</u>, and <u>be like</u> to succeed and thrive in this (each / all) arena / sphere of living? What must be our learner "exit / culminating" learner outcomes?*
5. *How might we analyze, clarify, and otherwise operationalize these general learner outcomes to the point that they can / will drive curriculum and instruction decisions?*
6. *Where does each of our State Standards fit within this listing / outline of "enabling" learner outcomes?*
7. *How do learners best learn each of the "enabling" learner outcomes?*
8. *What is our vision for a learning system that will allow each learner to be met at his / her personal learning level each day, and to demonstrate all enabling and culminating outcomes in the optimum period of time, a vision that considers our most basic research regarding student motivation and learning?*
9. *What are the infrastructure requirements for this organizational vision to become a reality?*
10. *How do we make our vision a reality? How do we plan and initiate change? More specifically, how do we create a need for change, help everyone to know how change will affect them personally, create a commitment to the change, create the capacity to change, and create a support system for the change?*

So now, more detail on each significant question:

Strategic Design Question # 1:

Do school systems exist to get students ready for life or to get ready for more school?

We have a strong bias on this first, and probably most important, question. We believe that schools exist to get learners ready for life. We also believe that the question does not have to be an either/or question. Learners can be prepared for both life and more school at the same time, but getting learners ready for life has to be the driver, the first thought, the primary decision screen. Today public (and private) schools are almost totally focused on getting "students" ready for more school. Educators might not want to admit that, might not even think about it, but our words and behaviors make it very clear. That reality becomes clear when present practices are contrasted with the Strategic Design questions and the Strategic Design planning process.

So question #1 is a go/no go question for Schwahn Leadership Associates. We choose to work only with school systems that put "life" before "more school" and embrace those that think/know that we can do both simultaneously. The why and how of choosing the both/and option will become clear throughout the remainder of this chapter and the remainder of this book.

We pride ourselves on being flexible, so taking the hard stand on the first question seems out of character as we tell about our bias. Reality is that when we explain our rationale for "preparing learners for life" and describe the process we use to help them make decisions, every system we have worked with agrees with our position. Maybe it's because the option of preparing learners for life has never been put in front of them, has never even been considered.

To bring this basic "purpose" question to the front, we only contract to facilitate the Strategic Design process with a system after we have been allowed to explain our rationale and describe the planning process. Here is how it goes. We ask for two hours with the Board of Education (and anyone else the Board might want to invite) and two hours with the Leadership Team (we require that all school principals be part of the presentation and discussion). We ask both the Board and the Leadership Team not to make their decision about contracting with us until we have exited. We don't want anyone to be pressured by our presence. We ask them to inform us of their decision in a few days. We are 100% on our clients' acceptance of the both/and decision in which the "Learning for Life" takes the high rung with "ready for more school" also being given high priority.

A closing note here for question #1. If you believe that your school system exists for getting students ready for more school, then you really don't need a strategic plan to implement that purpose. What you do need is 1) a strong textbook selection committee that values rigor, and 2) a strong focus on your state's learner standards. Past that, with sound management, your system can continue to operate as it has in the past. Our schools were designed by the *Committee of Ten* to prepare students to be successful university students more than 110 years ago, and neither the curriculum nor the instructional delivery system of our schools have changed much since then.

Strategic Design Question # 2:

In what arenas do successful adults live their lives; what are the basic spheres of living?

If "learning for life" is the purpose of school, then we have a purpose that might be a bit hard to get our arms around. Where do we start? How do we operationalize that fuzzy concept labeled "life?" At this point in the Strategic Design (SD) process, we ask participants to form small groups (usually about 6 to 8 people) to identify the arenas in which we live our lives. We give the total group an example or two and ask individuals and groups to reflect on where they live their lives; if they were to compartmentalize their lives, what might those compartments be called?

When we were first doing SD planning, we started from scratch on this question. After three or four times through the process we found that there were arenas/spheres of living that were common to all groups. We now save group time by providing a generic template for the arenas/spheres and ask the groups to modify it to meet the beliefs, values, and vocabulary of their community.

You might find it interesting to answer this question yourself, about you, before you continue. If you choose to do that, we suggest that you avoid peaking at (cheating, if you would) the diagram that follows. It was a fun activity for us the first time we considered the question.

Groups might use different vocabularies and labels, but most communities come to consensus around the following seven arenas/spheres of living, roughly defined by the following chart.

Significant Spheres of Living: In What Arenas Do We Spend Our Lives

- *Personal*:   Physical, Mental, Emotional, Social, Spiritual
- *Learning*:   Formal (Universities), Informal (Experiential)
- *Relationships*:   Intimate, Family, Work, Acquaintances
- *Economic*:   Worker, Consumer, Financial Manager
- *Civic*:   Political (Leaders, Issues, Directions), Obligations (Orderly Society, Contribution)
- *Global*:   Interrelationships (Economic, Political, Social), Environment
- *Cultural*:   Lifestyle, Heritage, Traditions, Values, the Arts (Literature, Music, Art, Dance)

These Arenas/Spheres of Living can be communicated in the following visual that provides the seven labels but also, to some degree, shows the relationship between the spheres.

This might be a good time to focus on the logic of the Strategic Design process and the Ten Questions. So listen for the logic: *If schools are preparing*

learners for life, then where do they live their lives . . . in the spheres of living. If we can identify those things that help people to live successful lives in each of these spheres, identify the knowledge, skills, and attitudes that help to ensure success in each sphere, and create a curriculum and instructional delivery system that ensures that each learner has acquired the knowledge, skills, and attitudes that will bring him/her success, we will be organized and aligned to send learners out the door "empowered to succeed in a rapidly changing world."

Mission Statement

Note: Today's leadership and change literature typically uses the word "mission" rather than "purpose" when labeling the reason the organization exists, the business it is in. We like the mission label. Mission sounds more like action than does purpose, more exciting, vital, and motivating. More like NASA and Mission Impossible.

When organizations write/finalize their Strategic Design, their mission is at the top. After all, it is the first and most general statement of the organization's direction. Although we agree with this placement in the written or digitized SD document, we find that identifying/creating it is best approached after the planning group has identified the spheres of living and the future conditions that accompany each sphere. We have an effective process for helping a group of 100 gain consensus around a mission statement, but the explanation of that process is too lengthy to describe in detail here. In short, we help the total group to identify the purpose/mission of their system. Basic criteria for an effective Mission Statement are that it be:

☑ *A statement of purpose and not a slogan.*

☑ *Exciting, motivating, meaningful.*

☑ *Clear, concise, sticky, easily memorized . . . 10 words or less.*

☑ *A statement with the power to drive the entire strategic design.*

We share a few of our favorite examples of good mission statements with the group to get them thinking in line with the above criteria. It's always a bit of fun to put mission statements in front of the group and ask participants to guess to whom the mission statement might belong. You might want to give the following a try.

10:30

Making People Independent Again
Producing World-Class ENGINES *and* DRIVE-TRAINS
Empowering All Learners to Succeed in a Rapidly
Changing World

(Key: Fed Ex, a rehab hospital, Honda, a public school)
Let's take a closer look at the power of #4, the public school vision:

Empowering All Learners to Succeed in a Rapidly Changing World

"empowering"	not "providing an opportunity to learn," not just educating or equipping, but empowering our graduates to be in control of their lives
"all learners"	not just the top quartile, not only those who come from good homes, but "all"
"to succeed"	succeed in relationships, careers, financially, spiritually
"in a rapidly changing world"	about continuous learning, future-focusing, being flexible, embracing meaningful change

Strategic Design Question # 3:

What are the future conditions in each of the arenas /
spheres of living, what will life be like, what will be the
challenges and opportunities?

It isn't strategic unless it is future focused. So what will the future conditions look like, to the best of our study, in each of the spheres of living? To facilitate getting the planning group to think "future," we ask them to read a paper that we have created and which we update about every 18 months entitled *The Future IS Now*. We read ten to fifteen futurist books each year and synthesize our notes into an easy to read document of about 20 pages. Participants are divided into "sphere" groups and identify the future conditions that they believe/think will have the greatest impact on that sphere of living. The following is an example of the future conditions identified by one of our groups for the "Personal" sphere of living.

Future Conditions of the <u>Personal</u> Sphere of Living

- The speed of change is rapid, continuous, and impactful.
- Individuals are faced with a steady stream of decisions, many with moral and ethical considerations.
- Continuous advances in communication technology significantly impact our personal life.
- Life's demands create time poverty and stress.
- Expectations are that products and services will be customized for the individual.
- We live in a 24/7 world where most commerce can take place at any time.
- There is an increased awareness of one's personal responsibility for a healthy lifestyle.
- Responsibility for financial long-term independence has moved from employers to individuals.
- Our rapidly changing world creates great opportunity for creative and motivated individuals.

Strategic Design Question # 4:

Given these future conditions in this (each) sphere of living, what will our graduates have to know, be able to do, and be like to succeed and thrive in this (each/all) arena/sphere of living. What must be our "exit, culminating" learner outcomes?

Question #4 is quite self-explanatory. If these are the conditions, the challenges, the opportunities that will exist in this sphere of living, what must we do to help our graduates succeed in this real world? The following is an example of how the group that identified the future conditions of the "Personal Sphere of Living" answered the question.

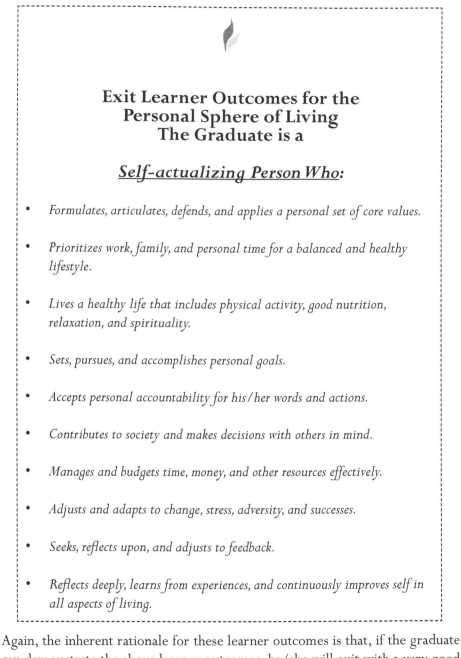

Exit Learner Outcomes for the Personal Sphere of Living
The Graduate is a

Self-actualizing Person Who:

• *Formulates, articulates, defends, and applies a personal set of core values.*

• *Prioritizes work, family, and personal time for a balanced and healthy lifestyle.*

• *Lives a healthy life that includes physical activity, good nutrition, relaxation, and spirituality.*

• *Sets, pursues, and accomplishes personal goals.*

• *Accepts personal accountability for his/her words and actions.*

• *Contributes to society and makes decisions with others in mind.*

• *Manages and budgets time, money, and other resources effectively.*

• *Adjusts and adapts to change, stress, adversity, and successes.*

• *Seeks, reflects upon, and adjusts to feedback.*

• *Reflects deeply, learns from experiences, and continuously improves self in all aspects of living.*

Again, the inherent rationale for these learner outcomes is that, if the graduate can demonstrate the above learner outcomes, he/she will exit with a very good chance of living a successful, happy, and contributing "Personal" life. Each of the Spheres of Living will contain learner outcomes of this nature.

Strategic Design Question # 5:

How might we analyze, clarify, and otherwise operationalize these general learner outcomes to the point that they can / will drive curriculum and instruction decisions?

Question #5 is not answered in the Strategic Planning group. This is where the curriculum and instruction people, with heavy involvement from department chairs and teachers, take over . . . and their tasks will significantly change their traditional job descriptions. They are now concerned with "preparation for life" rather than getting students ready for more school.

Let's take a closer look at the first bulleted learner outcome for the Personal Sphere of Living:

Formulates, articulates, defends, and applies a personal set of core values.

Is that a critical learner outcome for one's personal life? Can't get more "critical" than that! Where, when, and how is that critical outcome taught now with our present approach to curriculum and instruction? Might we not be very organized about what it is, how we teach it, and what the learner must do to show evidence of mastery? Might we expect that they will "get it as we go along?" Might we actually be "winging it?"

If this is to be a "culminating" outcome for our graduates, what might be our "enabling" outcomes? Where and when will they be studied and learned? How might this impact early childhood teachers, high school AP learning opportunities?

Strategic Design Question # 6:

Where does each of our State Standards fit within this listing / outline of "enabling" learner outcomes?

State standards are here, they are real, and they can't and shouldn't be dismissed. Thoughtful professionals created them. So where do they fit? Do we run one system for State Standards and another for our life-role learner outcomes? These are questions that we always get, and should get, when we help school systems create learner-centered strategic plans.

The task for the curriculum and instruction people is to find where those standards mesh with the life-role learner outcomes. From our experiences, we find that most State Standards easily match an exit (culminating) learner outcome or they fit nicely as "enabling" learner outcomes. It's about meshing and synthesizing, not about theirs and ours. It's also about synergy as the life-role learner outcomes bring a rationale for the learning and the Standards bring much of the basics.

Strategic Design Question # 7:

How do learners best learn each of the "enabling" learner outcomes?

This is the question that breaks with habit and tradition. Today, the question is thought and stated as "How should we teach that, or how *do* we teach that?" If the system is learner (client/customer) centered, the question has to be "How do learners best learn that?"

The way this question is answered is also critical from an instructional delivery/**MCL** point of view. If the answer to the "how best learned" question is "online with a computer," much of the teacher's valuable time and expertise can be saved for those learner outcomes that require interaction, conflict, problem solving, and coaching.

Strategic Design Question # 8:

What is our vision for a learning system that will allow each learner to be met at his/her personal learning level each day, and to demonstrate all enabling and culminating outcomes in the optimum period of time; a vision that considers our most basic research regarding student motivation and learning?

This question is BIG. For the answer must take us from a bureaucracy to a service orientation, from our assembly line system for instructional delivery to mass customized learning, and from the Industrial Age to the Age of Empowerment. Chapter 4, "*Through the Learner's Eyes*" begins to answer this question. Chapter 6, "*MCL: The Vision (Detailed)*" and Chapter 7, "*Lori Does Her Learning Schedule*" are dedicated to describing and operationalizing a MASS CUSTOMIZED LEARNING vision.

Strategic Design Question # 9:

What are the infrastructure requirements for this organizational vision to become a reality?

Chapter 8, "*Weight Bearing Walls,*" and Chapter 9, "*Ready for Rollout*" answer this question and create new job descriptions for everyone at the District Office. Creating the **MCL** infrastructure is the "heavy lifting" part of transforming schools from the Industrial Age to the Information Age.

Strategic Design Question # 10:

How do we make our vision a reality? How do we plan and initiate change? More specifically, how do we create a need for change, help everyone to know how change will affect them personally, create a commitment to the change, create the capacity to change, and create a support system for the change?

This is the leadership question. Our final chapter, Chapter 10, "*Total Leaders*" is about how leaders must think, what they must value, and what they must do to make the MASS CUSTOMIZED LEARNING Vision a reality. This chapter is mostly about Strategic Direction. Chapter 10 is about the change process, managing the vision, and Strategic Alignment. **MCL** is about true, comprehensive, systemic, and transformational change. Behavior doesn't change unless structure changes. There is power and efficiency in organizational alignment.

Note: Schwahn and Spady's companion books for AASA titled _Total Leaders 2.0_ and _Learning Communities 2.0_, published in 2010 are excellent resources for understanding leadership and how to apply the Total Leaders Framework to the transformation of school systems.

Chapter 3
Takeaways:

The mission, the purpose of education, must be to prepare students for the challenges and opportunities they will encounter after they leave school. Students must also be prepared for more schooling, but that is not the first or only purpose of public education.

Educators must be logical, must provide a tight rationale for what learners must know, be able to do, and be like in order to succeed in a rapidly changing world. We can't just continue our outdated thinking, processes, and structures. Habit and tradition must give way to future-focusing and visionary leadership.

Creating modern and effective school systems in a logical fashion requires planners to ask the right questions, apply their study of the future, and be prepared to make significant and meaningful change.

Chapter 4

Through the Learner's Eyes

*"Successful businesses view their products and services
through the eyes of their customers
....and design their organizational structure accordingly."*

*"Successful school systems view their learning opportunities
through the eyes of learners
.....and design their instructional delivery system accordingly."*

Chuck Schwahn

🖋

Chapter 4 Intent

To bring sharp focus on the learner and learning experience when planning, designing, and creating learning communities. To identify today's learners…who they are, how they are different, and what they bring with them. In short, to become learner centered and future focused in how we think, make decisions, and act.

Note: *This chapter is somewhat of a fantasy, and will feel like that to "in-the-box" thinkers. But before you finish Inevitable: MCL, you will know this fantasy, THIS VISION, to be entirely possible, probable, and yes…..Inevitable.*

As you put together the last four "how to" chapters of Inevitable, you will see that this chapter, "Through the Learner's Eyes" is desirable, exciting, and… doable.

Digital Natives and Digital Immigrants

We label those born after 1990 as Digital Natives. They were born digital. They have never experienced anything but a digital world. We think of anyone who remembers IBM typewriters, white out, letters typed and sent via the US mail, news at 5:30 PM, telephone cords, handwritten receipts, and athletes who didn't gloat, as Digital Immigrants. Now to be fair, we quickly admit that there are many Digital Immigrants who have learned that second language, but for most of us, it has been a rather long and relatively flat learning curve . . . and we still speak with a bit of an accent. Digital is the Digital Natives' first language. Did little Bobby say "iPod" or "Mommy" first?

The technology of the last decade has changed everything. Now that statement might be too strong, but we think that it is more accurate than to say it "changed many or most things." Technology has shifted a good deal of power from the Digital Immigrants to the Digital Natives. We have moved from "Father Knows Best" to "Hey Bobby, can you help me to find that financial webpage or whatever they call it;" from "Now where did I put that chicken enchilada recipe," to "Just a second, Mom, I'll Google it for you."

We suggest two books to help you to know who these Digital Natives are and how they think and operate. *Grown Up Digital* is Dan Tapscott's second book on the topic. About ten years ago, Tapscott introduced us to the digital world and its impact on our youth with _Growing up Digital_, and now, with _Grown Up Digital_, he has fast forwarded us to what the world looks like to those who have known nothing other than today's digital world. _Born Digital_, written by John Palfrey and Urs Gasser, covers much of the same territory as the title suggests, but the books are different enough and the topic is important enough to warrant reading both books. Interestingly, one author concludes that education need not change and the other believes transformational change is needed, and now. One is obviously ITB (that's in-the-box for those who don't text) and the other understands the "transformational" part of transformational technology. You get to guess who is who . . . just another incentive for you to read both books.

Living the Life of a Digital Native (DN)

> "_Today's kids are so bathed in bits that they think it's all part of the natural landscape, just another part of their environment._"
> **Palfrey and Gasser**

This above quote, in a general sense, says it all. But educators and parents will want and expect specifics that lead to a deeper understanding of the DN's ways of thinking, acting, and living. So, for now, to tide you over until you read the suggested books, allow us to make a few points about today's DNs, about today's learners, about today's students.

☑ Digits have always been part of the DN's environment. Ho Hum!

☑ DNs learned to manipulate technology early and have never been afraid of it. They haven't had to relearn anything. Having to use "white out" if they make a mistake is not a threat.

☑ There has been a bit of a role reversal as regards things digital . . . DNs are frequently their parents' teachers . . . and on occasion, their teachers' teachers.

☑ DNs are controlling markets and their cultural environment. The world is listening to them and giving them what they want.

☑ DNs expect interaction; they no longer accept one-way broadcasts. They are not only consumers of information; they are also creators of information.

☑ DNs are probably smarter and savvier than previous generations. (Now don't take that personally. You too are probably guilty of telling everyone how intelligent your grandkids are and how they manage the computer with ease. We plead guilty!)

☑ DNs will transform organizations, politics . . . and, inevitably, education.

☑ On the downside, the issue of privacy is the #1 concern of adult digital experts . . . but not the concern of many DNs.

"We are witnessing the Amazonification of libraries.
It's the research library vs Google and Wikipedia."
Palfrey and Gasser

Values and Expectations of the Digital Native

Tapscott nails this one. <u>Grown Up Digital </u>details the eight norms of the Net Generation. The norms ring true to your humble authors' experiences. (The following labels are from Tapscott, the trailers are ours.)

Freedom	*Freedom to do what they want, when they want, and with whom they want. This is not about being lazy or irresponsible. It is about doing what is personally meaningful at the time.*
Customization	*They expect personalization everywhere, and why not. Technology has made mass customization the norm. Except for public schools, of course. (See subtitle of <u>Inevitable</u>.)*
Scrutiny	*Yes, there are shysters out there in cyber world, but NetGeners have learned to spot them and, for the most part, not be taken in.*
Integrity	*It's a transparent world and the NetGeners expect leaders and organizations to act with integrity . . . even when they themselves justify illegally downloading music.*
Collaboration	*Social networks are their thing. Technology has made making and keeping "friends" easy. They love to communicate and prefer to work and learn in teams.*
Entertainment	*Everything should have an enjoyment component, work and learning included.*
Speed	*Expectations are that everything will be communicated and experienced in real time. Google knows what they want before they finish typing the second word of a four word request.*
Innovate	*The new new thing is expected. NetGeners live in the age of continuous discovery. It's hard to impress them with the latest gadget. If Jobs doesn't announce a new*

> *world-changing gizmo every January, Apple is thought to be on its way out.*

This may be a good spot to interject a request for reader reflection. Please give the following questions some serious thought.

> *How consistent and complementary are these NetGener norms with the structure, policies, and practices of public schools? If this is their life outside of school, what might be their assessment and evaluation of schools and schooling?*
>
> *If we were to restructure schools to take advantage of the technology that has created these NetGener norms, what might our learning institutions look like, feel like, and be like?*

Now that we have examined what learners bring with them to school, we would like to introduce you to the learners and take you through Lori's day of learning. The infrastructure necessary to make this day possible for Lori will be detailed in Chapters 7, 8, and 9, but we wanted to put the learner at the middle of our vision so that the focus is on the learner and learning and not on the technology that makes it all work. Technology is a critical tool, but the learner and learning is our core purpose . . . actually, our **only purpose**.

THE LEARNERS

Lori:

> *14 years old, parents are both educators, middle class*
> *Quite responsible . . . but a teenager*
> *Interested in pop music, athletics, math, and technology*
> *Knows that she is college bound*
> *Thinks that Christopher is "cool"*

Christopher:

> *14 years old, parents both in business, upper-middle class*
> *Talented, learning comes easy, but not that turned on by school*
> *Interested in sports, rock music, Calvin and Hobbs, and a "pro" career*
> *Talents fit the mold of an engineer*
> *College would be second choice to being in the Rockies farm system*
> *Thinks that Lori is kinda cute*

Lori's School Day, December 10, 2013

Background:

Lori lives with her parents in a small town of about 15,000. She is enrolled in a school system that in 2010 participated thoughtfully and enthusiastically in the Strategic Design process described in Chapter 3. The planning process resulted in an innovative, future-focused vision that the planning group chose to label MASS CUSTOMIZED LEARNING. Because their bold vision differed so strikingly from the traditional system that everyone had known for more than a century, the planning group agreed that changing its name from a "School District" to a "Learning Community" would be more appropriate and more descriptive.

> *6:30 a.m.: Lori's iPhone alarm lets her know that it's that time. She puts her finger on the iCal icon of her iPad, checks her schedule and gets ready for the day.*

No one else in the entire school system . . . excuse us, the entire Learning Community has Lori's exact schedule. Each learner (Oh yes, lest we forget, the teachers refer to students as "learners" because that's what they are, and they call themselves "learning facilitators" because that's what they do.) has a learning schedule based on his/her individual needs . . . his/her individual needs for that very day!

> *7:45 a.m.: Lori's "pick up time."*

The old "school bus system" has given way to a more flexible system for getting learners to where they need to go. Instead of all 50-passenger buses that get students to a central location by 8:15, the Learning Community (LC) now operates a service more similar to limos. Not the limos of stars, but the limos of regular passengers who need to get to airports. Transportation departments, rather than dictating starting and ending times, are now in the "learning business." They too are Mass Customizing their services.

Lori does not have to schedule her ride with the LC's transportation service, but she may. Parents might drop Lori off, she may walk, catch a ride with a friend, whatever. But regardless, learning is the dog and transportation is the tail.

> *8:00 a.m.: Lori is in the School Counselor's meeting room just in time for the start of her Interpersonal Communications Seminar. This is the second week of the seminar which runs from 8 to 11 each M-W-F morning.*

Interpersonal Communications (IPC) is an important "learner outcome" that is part of both the Personal and the Relationship Spheres of Living. Lori's seminar is participatory and hands on. To fulfill the requirements of the IPC seminar learning outcome, she will be required to effectively demonstrate

* paraphrasing	* describing feelings
* behavior description	* giving and receiving feedback
* perception checking	* communicating under pressure

Her learning facilitator is a true professional skilled at facilitating the IPC seminar. She has a good deal of experience. She facilitates this seminar 5 to 8 times each year and it is one of her favorites. Learners catch her enthusiasm and trust her expertise. She is a very professional learning facilitator, proud of her career choice.

Three of Lori's good girlfriends are also in this group of 15 IPC seminar participants . . . as is Christopher. Now HOW did this happen? By chance, by accident, by luck . . . or do these kids know something about how to manipulate a system?

> *11:15 a.m.: Lori has a short 30-minute meeting scheduled with her Learning Coach to review her schedule plans for the next two months.*

Although Lori has *earned* the right to create her own learning plan, she always appreciates the suggestions from her parents and her coach. All are aware that Lori is headed for college and make sure that her schedule and learner outcomes reflect the entrance requirements for the three or four universities that are on her wish list. Lori's coach is a person labeled as "one with the need to know" and therefore has real-time electronic notification of all of Lori's decisions, activities, and accomplishments. Lori's coach likes her to have some "face time" every two weeks or so . . . even if no one senses any problems.

All learning facilitators (formerly called teachers) are responsible for coaching from 12 to 15 learners. Although the LC has the final decision regarding who will coach specific learners, there is, as far as possible, an attempt to allow the learner the right to choose his/her coach. The learning coach is the final authority regarding the learner's schedule. Self-directed learners who have demonstrated the maturity necessary to plan their own schedule are encouraged to do so. The Learning Community (LC) is serious about creating lifelong learners and they expect all learners to reach that maturity before they graduate.

> *12:00 p.m.: Lori is "brown bagging" it for lunch today. She has a lunch meeting with a Bank Director who has agreed to mentor her through the creation of a business plan.*

Creating and defending a business plan is an outcome in the *Economic Sphere of Living*, and although Lori could have taken the seminar offered on that topic, she instead chose to fulfill the requirements of the Business Plan outcome by doing a special project. Her mentor at the bank was at one time a professional performer and Lori has a strong interest in learning about the economic realities of the music industry. The meeting will give Lori an opportunity to apply those Interpersonal Communication Skills that she was working on this morning.

Lori got some help on this one from her mom who knew some of the Bank Director's history. It is proving to be very positive for both Lori and her mentor. Lori is thrilled to learn what it's really like to be an entertainer, with a special emphasis on the $$$$$ part of it, and her mentor enjoys reliving her days as a struggling performer.

Lori's demonstration of her ability to Create and Defend a Business Plan will take the form of a presentation of her plan to the loan department of the bank. The bank will apply all of the criteria that they would normally apply to a loan request. Can't get much more authentic and real with learner assessment than that!

> *1:00 – 3:00 p.m.: Lori is in an online math and science cooperative learning group.*

Lori and three of her girlfriends have scheduled two hours four times a week when they can do their online math and science learning together. They could do their math individually but they like each other and doing math as a small group allows for peer coaching and socializing a bit. Lori and her team have set a goal that they will all be ready for college calculus as their first university math course. Today, they have chosen to meet in a small meeting room in the Learning Center (formerly the school) that they have reserved from 1 to 3 p.m.

The Learning Community ensures that each student has a Netbook computer and access to online learning. At about $300 for a quality Netbook, and with prices continuing to drop for most technology, many of the parents can afford the computer and those who can't are loaned one by the LC. The budget office has found that furnishing computers is less costly than the textbooks they used to buy. Bing and Google are available for web searches and Wikipedia seems to have pertinent information on nearly everything.

The curriculum and instruction team has put all learner outcomes that are efficiently and effectively learned online available on the LC's website 24/7. Most online instructional programs include online learner evaluations and those evaluations, those demonstrations of learning, are automatically added to their electronic learning portfolio. Lori's Learning Coach, her parents, and the LC records office all are informed of her progress in real time. Lori and her learning coach have set challenging expectations for her rate of progress, and both Lori and her coach are automatically signaled when those expectations are not met . . . but in fairness, a motivational "attagirl" is forthcoming when she meets those expectations. Isn't this technology just fun!!

> *3:30 – 5:00 p.m.: Lori is at the LC sports complex for gymnastics practice.*

Lori loves gymnastics. Nastia Liukin is a heroine. She has tapes of all of Nastia's Olympic performances and has modeled her moves after Nastia. Gymnastics practice is from 3:30 to 5 p.m. or so each day in the LC sports complex . . . which is also open in the early mornings and evenings to serve the community. Lori frequently catches a ride home with one of her parents after gymnastics. When schedules don't mesh, she rides the bus provided by the LC that serves the learners who are participating in LC related sports activities.

Lori has "grown up digital." She has never known a world without computers, the Internet, iPods, and cell phones. She mostly lives in a paperless world . . . doesn't bring home books as everything she needs is available online. She is totally at ease with the social networks of the day. Loves keeping in touch with her friends. Is an excellent texter . . . a true member of the "thumb generation." All day long, whenever there is the opportunity, Lori checks in with her friends to learn what they are doing, what's happening, who said what about whom, where they might meet tonight or over the weekend.

Right now is an interesting time for Lori on Facebook. As with most seminars, Lori's learning facilitator has created a "friends list" for her IPC seminar groups and Lori is eager to find what is posted . . . by her friends or by her learning facilitator. She finds a fun entry from YouTube demonstrating how not to "communicate feelings," (hitting is not appropriate) and another on how to "demand request an increase in your allowance." The video suggests that if you want a "yes" for an answer, you must ask a "yesable" question. So maybe the request should include a "perception check" to determine what Dad might expect from you in return for that additional Lincoln. Lori's learning facilitator also has posted an interesting theory paper titled *Avoiding Defensive Communication*.

6:00 – 8:00 p.m. or so: Dinner time and family conversation.

Sitting down with the family for a meal when everyone has a busy schedule these days is difficult, but Lori's parents try to make it happen as often as possible. Might the table conversation be about that "defensive communication" thing? Sounds a bit like the Cleavers, right?

Lori is scheduled to begin a seminar titled "Diversity: Strength or Detractor" in about a week. The "Diversity" seminar is part of both the *Civic Sphere of Living* and the *Economic Sphere*. When she placed her request for the seminar she was informed that there was a reading requirement for admission. The seminar addresses the issue of racism and race relations, and the seminar facilitators wanted to ensure that learners had some background on that issue.

Lori has the choice to study the Civil War, the history of Western Expansion in the US, or the history of blacks and professional sports. The seminar leaders have identified three or four books in each of the three categories and have asked participants to be diverse in their readings so that many perspectives can be described to the seminar group. Lori has chosen a book titled <u>Bury My Heart at Wounded Knee</u> because of her father's childhood experiences. Christopher has chosen to read a biography of Jackie Robinson because of his interest in sports and especially baseball.

Yes, you are right, what a coincidence . . . Lori and Christopher have again manipulated the system so that they are in this same seminar. They just might be showing some basic talents that could lead to careers in politics, law, or marketing.

> *8:30 p.m.: Lori wonders if she should read about General Custer and Little Big Horn or if she should give Christopher a call to discuss "the subtle Interpersonal Communication Skill of Describing Feelings" with him . . . too bold? What might he think? Heck, why not, this isn't the 00s you know!*

> *9:30 p.m.: Lori plugs her iPhone and her Netbook in for a charge, checks for text messages, finds four, answers two, sets her alarm for tomorrow. It has been a good day. Everything she did had a purpose. She could relate all of her activities of the day to her future . . . her future as a learner and her future as a contributing member of society. She is motivated to go after it again in the morning.*

More than 50% of the learner outcomes that Lori is required to demonstrate (learning outcomes are demonstrations of learning) can be effectively and efficiently learned online. Typically Lori spends about two hours a day by herself working through her enabling outcomes. She can do that work at any time from anyplace. It might be from home, from a friend's home, maybe even from Starbucks or another hotspot hangout.

But......

What if Lori were not a responsible fourteen-year-old?

What if she didn't have the motivation to work when no one was watching?

What if she couldn't be trusted?

Motivation, Maturity, and Supervision

It might be easy for you, the reader, to see Lori's behavior portrayed as being Pollyanna and dismiss what could become the maturity/responsibility norm for young learners. Well, it isn't. Lori is a real person and her maturity runs well ahead of the above portrayal. Moreover, the three friends whom Lori tends to run with, play with, and work with are equally mature and responsible. So is Christopher, by the way. We find that maturity is a rather natural thing if it is intentionally taught, expected, and rewarded.

When children and young adults are always/mostly told what to do, when to do it, how to do it, and then watched closely to make sure they have done it, why should we expect a natural increase in maturity and acceptance of responsibility? High school students frequently are directed even more than are kindergarteners. For proof of that, spend a couple of hours in a Kindergarten classroom and then watch a couple of Algebra I classes.

> ***Quick Story (cjs):*** *I vividly recall a friend telling what happened at the dinner table the evening before he and his wife were to take their daughter, a beautiful and talented 18-year-old, to the university to begin her life away from home. His story was to make a point. He was sincere and somewhat sad about the brief interchange between his wife and daughter. Near the end of the meal, his wife looked at their daughter's plate and then at their daughter and said, "Emily, finish your peas."*

Maybe we should leave that story right there. Maybe it doesn't need explanation given the topic of this section. But of course we can't! The following day, Emily would be making all of her decisions. When to get up, whom to befriend, how hard to work, whom she might date, whether or not she would drink, smoke, do drugs . . . . and this evening we felt it necessary to tell her to "eat her peas."

MASS CUSTOMIZED LEARNING begins creating responsible, self-directed, lifelong learners from day one. And **MCL** gives educators a big head start. Is learning natural? Do five-year-olds come to us highly motivated to learn? Well yes, a LOUD YES if you would! So what happens sometime and somewhere between that first day and about March of grade 4? Our take is that learning can and will remain intrinsically motivating if three conditions are continuously met:

1. If learners are consistently met at their learning level.

If the learning is challenging and the learner continues to expect to succeed. Don't expect me to be good at Algebra II when I received a C- in Algebra I. Don't expect me to be turned on to Sally, Dick, and Jane when I am reading the sports page every day to learn how the Broncos are doing.

2. If learners are allowed to learn in their natural learning styles.

Demonstrate, let me watch, let me try it, give me feedback, coach and I will get it . . . but learning by listening to lectures doesn't work well for me. Now my friend Bob is just the opposite.

3. If learners are allowed to learn while using a content of interest.

Racism is more interesting to Lori when she thinks of how Native Americans were and continue to be perceived and treated. Christopher will relate to Jackie Robinson's struggles and courage as the first Black in the major leagues or George Wallace, Governor of Alabama, attempting to deny the entrance of Black students to the University of Alabama.

Our present system that puts 25-30 students with one teacher doesn't allow for any of these three critical motivators. **MCL** allows true professionals to apply all three of these powerful intrinsic motivators simultaneously, for everyone, every hour of every day. You will learn how in Chapters 6 through 9.

But What About Little Johnny?

Learners don't learn at the same rate and kids don't mature and learn to take responsibility at the same rate. So what? Madeline Hunter made a paradigm shifting statement when, after her presentation on the topic of "Individualizing Instruction," she was asked, "At what age are children ready for Kindergarten?" Dr. Hunter kindly and gently said, "That's the wrong question . . . the question is 'What is the child ready for?'" Madeline . .and Chuck did get to know her quite well so she did become "Madeline" . . . helped move us from school centered to learner centered, from bureaucrat to professional with that one true and timely statement.

So the right question is, "What type of supervision/control is Johnny ready for?" **MCL** allows for personalizing the responsibility factor as well as the intrinsic motivators listed above. **MCL** is intentional about creating self-directed, lifelong learners; it is a focus from the beginning. If learners aren't their own pilots able to demonstrate most of the criteria for the Learning Sphere of Living by the time they are 15 or 16, there is cause for concern.

Note: *Later we will talk about empowerment . . . but for now, just know that to be empowered, one must be a self-directed, lifelong learner. Know also that empowered people produce, in the workplace and in the Learning Community. And finally, know that empowered people require little supervision. Follow the line here. This "empowerment thing" is great for the supervisor. Empowered people take much less of your, the supervisor's/ teacher's time; time that can be spent elsewhere.*

But for now, what if Johnny is fourteen and has not seen the light?

Lori was able to plan her schedule and simply get it approved by her parents and her learning coach. Lori actually ran the "scheduling" meeting.

> *The learning facilitator will chair this meeting with Johnny and his parent(s) and assign Johnny tasks and responsibilities.*

Lori needed to report to her learning coach only every couple of weeks or so and the meeting was usually quite short.

> *Johnny may have to check in each day to review his activities and accomplishments with his learning coach.*

Lori can work online from anywhere at any time.

> *Johnny will do his online work, which was determined by his learning coach, in the computer lab, the library, or any specific place that is monitored by someone with authority.*

Lori can choose her after-hours activities.

Johnny will be given homework assignments.

In short, there will be a task orientation for all learners. That task orientation hopefully will be applied by the learner himself/herself, but if not, the LC will apply the task orientation. Not as a punitive thing, but as a necessary thing, a temporary thing, all the while working with Johnny to help him become a responsible, empowered, self-directed, lifelong learner. No one wins until Johnny has become his own "learning" pilot. Everyone wins when he does.

Serious About Lifelong Learning?

One of the significant Spheres of Living identified in the LC's Strategic Design is the Learning Sphere. The following is a real example of the Learning Sphere exit outcome for a school system with which we have worked. This exit learner outcome is the creation of a Strategic Design planning group made up of approximately 100 people from all significant school and community role groups.

We insert this important set of learner outcomes here so that you might see how consistent Lori's scheduling process is with her becoming a Self-Directed, Lifelong Learner.

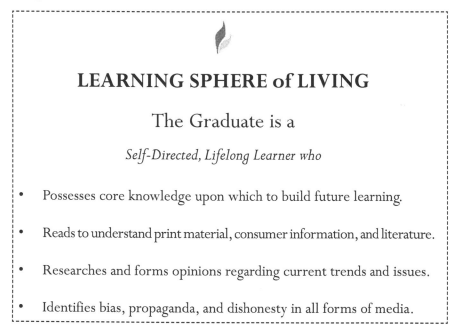

LEARNING SPHERE of LIVING

The Graduate is a

Self-Directed, Lifelong Learner who

- Possesses core knowledge upon which to build future learning.

- Reads to understand print material, consumer information, and literature.

- Researches and forms opinions regarding current trends and issues.

- Identifies bias, propaganda, and dishonesty in all forms of media.

- Creates and pursues purposeful and challenging learning goals.

- Acquires, organizes, analyzes, evaluates, and synthesizes information from a wide variety of sources and applies that information to solve problems.

- Takes advantage of learning opportunities created by technological advances.

- Shares his/her learning with others by teaching and modeling.

- Transfers learning and successful practices to new situations.

- Seeks learning opportunities consistent with future-focused vision of self.

If it is important, it should be intentional.
Stephen Covey

Finding Our Passion

In 2007 Rick Warren's *The Purpose Driven Life* was everywhere, #1 on the book bestseller lists, DVD lists, and a sure hit on talk shows. Warren seems to have ridden a wave that comes with many labels. Other self-help gurus have called the wave "meaningful work, engagement, drive, being in the zone, in the flow, conscious living, self-fulfillment, etc. etc." Although economic times (2009) have made life difficult for many as we write *Inevitable,* generally, the lives of Americans have mostly been that of abundance. When abundance replaces "I do what I have to do to make it," we are allowed to think more about things like purpose and meaning and less about things like "feeding my family" and "I can't wait for the weekend."

Ken Robinson's book titled *The Element* brought the "Purposeful Life" wave together for us. Although Robinson's wisdom is for all ages, it has a special ring for how finding one's passion could help young learners get a head start with creating a meaningful life . . . which just may be the ultimate intrinsic motivator. This message is just as relevant for parents and grandparents as it is for educators. Get the book, give it a read; 'tis well worth the time.

Robinson in _The Element_, that book you are going to read, says that we are:

> . . . in our element, in our zone, in the flow
> (think Michael Jordan, think Shawn Johnson, think Steve Jobs)
> when our passion intersects with our strongest talents.

So, the message to YOU! Why not **intentionally** help, encourage, and coach our students/learners, our children, our grandchildren to "find their passion?" MASS CUSTOMIZED LEARNING allows the flexibility for learners to check out a number of possibilities while working through their "getting ready for life" program.

Stephen Covey taught us that, "anything important should be intentional." Living a meaningful life is about as important as it gets. Knowing, cultivating, and capitalizing on the intersection of one's passions and talents is the staging.

The following short, sad-but-true story makes our point:

**A Story (cjs):** My older brother, a capable, responsible and intelligent guy, was an electrician, mostly wiring homes and small businesses for all of his working life. He was good at what he did, one of the best, never wanted for work, always satisfied customers. He and his wife raised a beautiful family. All four kids are college grads, all excellent parents, salt of the earth kind of people. That's the good news. The not so good news .. . he retired at 64, and about a year after his retirement I had occasion to talk with him about his new life.

"Well, what do you think about this retirement thing?""It's great, really great. I worked for 45 years and I hated every damn day of it."
All said with the most sincere and believable look on his face that the world has known.

Again, this is another case where maybe we should leave it right here, we have made our point, YOU GET IT! But of course we can't. He wasted a big portion of his life hating it.

> **Continued (cjs):** *His brother (who will also remain nameless) wanted to play college basketball and so enrolled in a "teachers college" because a couple of his buddies were going there, it was a state school with cheap tuition, and they had a good basketball program . . . it was all about basketball with no intention of graduating. Kids from South Dakota Lakota reservations typically didn't graduate from college. But lo and behold he surprised everyone, including himself, by becoming a fairly good student. Because it was a teachers college, he graduated with teaching credentials and started a career in the world's most important profession. What a break! What a LUCKY break! A break that helped create a "Purposeful Life," and provide work that he "loved every damn day." Well, almost every day.*

So two brothers, otherwise quite similar, have very different lives. Both successful by others' standards but, from inside, their work couldn't have been more different. Much luck was involved in these two lives. The brothers were both taking what life was giving them one day at a time. Neither very conscious of the impact of what then seemed rather insignificant decisions. Let us repeat the Covey truism . . . "If it's important, it should be intentional." Put that Covey statement on your mental hard drive. It is some of the best advice ever and should be applied daily – to almost everything. Like in, "Did I tell Genny that I love her?"

Age of Empowerment

We all know and mostly understand the Agrarian Age, the Industrial Age, and the Information Age, but we're not sure how to label the age in which we are now living. About ten years ago our colleague, Bill Spady, the world analysis and synthesis champion, suggested that we were living in the Age of Continuous Discovery. And who could argue. New technology was being discovered by the week . . . to the point that nothing seemed to amaze. The Internet. Ho hum. The iPod. Ho hum. The cell phone. Ho hum. eBay. Ho hum. YouTube. Ho hum. And it hasn't stopped. Nor will it.

Trouble with naming Ages these days is that they come faster, are more complex, and exit faster all the time. Futurists could see the Industrial Age coming, we could all get used to it, and it hung around an entire lifetime plus. Schwahn (ahem) and Spady, in their 2010 book titled _Learning Communities 2.0_, labeled today's age as the Age of Empowerment. Remember ten years ago or so when the word "empowerment" hit the leadership and change literature and most of us thought that it was nothing more than a new word for "delegation" that would exit with little fanfare in a short time. Well, it hasn't left. It is not "delegation." We now know that empowered people PRODUCE BIG TIME.

Our quick definition for "empowerment" is:

Putting people in control of the variables that they perceive important to their success.

Note that empowerment is not what _we_ think is important to their success, but what _they_ perceive to be important. In other words, empowerment is in the eyes, feelings, and attitudes of the empowered. When applied from this definition, it is quite easy to see why empowered people produce. Empowered people find meaning in their work, they are engaged, they are intrinsically motivated.

MCL is empowering to the learner as a learner while, at the same time, building in the skills, attitudes, and habits of empowerment for life after graduation. Stated a bit differently, **MCL** is the "empowerment model" of education/ learning. Empowered workers produce! Empowered learners learn! The following one-to-one comparisons help to make the point.

EMPOWERMENT	MASS CUSTOMIZED LEARNING
Clear Goals	Learner Outcomes
Layout of Own Work	Choose Our Learning Style & Content of Interest
Empowering Technologies	Online Learning and Scheduling Technologies
Customer / Client Centered	Learner Centered
Meaningful Work	Learning Relevant to Life
Engaged Workers	Motivated Learners

Chapter 4
Takeaways:

Today's learners bring very different experiences and expectations with them. Schools that were structured for a different age cannot be expected to meet the learning needs of the NetGeners.

Students and learning must be the focus of today's "learning communities." Bureaucratic, administratively convenient, control-oriented systems will not and cannot meet the needs of our learners, our society, or our nation. There IS a better way and we can see it!

If our graduates are to leave our schools as "Self-Directed, LifeLong Learners," we must be intentional about creating that attitude and those habits.

Chapter 5

About Learning: The Baby and the Bathwater

"Every gambler knows
that the secret to survival is
knowing what to throw away, and
knowing what to keep."

"The Gambler," Kenny Rogers

"Don't throw the baby out with the bathwater."

(Not sure on this one, but we think our Moms said it first)

Chapter 5 Intent

**To challenge educators to apply our most basic
research/knowledge about
learning and learners and about effective organizations.
Said another way,
to challenge education and educators to move
from an industry concerned with administrative convenience
to a profession concerned with the personal needs of
clients/learners.**

We begin Chapter 5 with one of our attributes of professionalism:

A professional "acts on/applies the research base of the profession."

The research base of education is clear and robust. Meta-analyses conducted by the giants of educational research (Benjamin Bloom, Madeline Hunter, Robert Marzano, Edward Deci, Larry Lezotte, John Hattie, and others) have helped us to understand:

*how human beings learn ... and
the conditions under which human beings learn best*

Upon reading their conclusions and works, we often respond as a little guy in our family who used to say when presented with something *new*, "Know dat!" Yes, often the conclusions from 35 years of educational research elicit an "I kinda knew that" from us. The irony is: practices and procedures in schools and in classrooms are often not congruent with the research...with what we know. It is as if we are *pretending not to know*....**pretending** not to know that:

√ *Humans learn in different ways.*

√ *There are many ways to be intelligent.*

√ *Humans learn in different time frames.*

√ *Well, we could go on and on....*and be sure, we WILL later!

Principles….Not Beliefs

With great fanfare and consensus these research conclusions often find their way into belief statements articulated in school communities around our country. No doubt the two most popular statements hailed are:

We believe students learn in different ways, and
We believe students learn in different time frames.

However, calling these statements "beliefs" is a misnomer. These are not beliefs. "Beliefs" imply choice, options, opinions:

Some of us believe _____.
The rest of us do not believe _____.

…..and the implication is that THAT'S okay. We can agree to disagree, to believe different things.

But these statements are not statements of beliefs. Rather, they are <u>principles</u>, they have their root in our most basic research regarding students and learning. Math and science folks know exactly what we mean when we say "principles." These statements are *grounded in the research*. They are the proven "rules" which *should* guide the work. They are not opinions. They are nonnegotiables.

Rarely do statements of principle become the screen or guide for our decisions and practices. Instead, they are often relegated to a cabinet or to a page in the Strategic Planning notebook, or they become wall hangings – sometimes beautifully done in calligraphy or better yet cross-stitch. Okay, we admit hyperbole here, but you get the message!

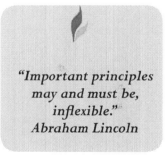

"Important principles may and must be, inflexible."
Abraham Lincoln

These statements, these principles, proven in the research, need to determine <u>what we DO</u> and <u>how we DO IT</u>. Further, and equally important if we want to make it possible for teachers to implement these principles, the structure of the organization must be <u>aligned with and supportive of the PRINCIPLES</u>.

Form Follows Function

A little story about "form and function" might help illustrate this point.

> **A Quick Story (bmcg):** *A few years ago, my husband, Dick, and I decided that our house needed a facelift. Truth be told, it started with my wanting to replace the kitchen sink and to paint the previously stained woodwork throughout the house, both of which were met with resistance from Dick for a number of reasons obvious to most husbands. Undeterred and armed with strategies only wives understand (which included words like "resale" and "equity"), my earlier wants grew into a full-blown house facelift. Collaboratively — yes, collaboratively!, we identified a list of needs and wants which included (not surprising to those who know us) a garage system that would hide 700+ lobster traps and a closet system that would house an equal number of pairs of shoes! Overwhelmed by translating those needs and wants into actual structural changes, we sought the help of our friend, Marilyn, also a gifted architect. The phrase "form follows function" comes to mind. The structure, the design, the form of anything should be determined by the functional needs. Our list of needs and wants became our function stuff. Marilyn, in true creative genius, translated our function stuff into a beautiful structure....Thus, the form was dictated by the function. We love the result. Meets our needs, makes it easy to live our ideal life, looks great.*

In education, principles, such as these, define our <u>FUNCTION</u>:

> *Students learn in different ways.*
> *Student learn in different time frames.*

And everything WE DO and HOW WE DO IT (the <u>FORM</u>) should be designed from our function statements:

√ how we teach learners

√ how we assess them

√ how we give them feedback

√ how we credential them

√ how we structure the organization etc., etc., etc.

Yet, our Industrial Age delivery system does not allow us to design learning congruent with those principles which we so enthusiastically espouse. Instead of leapfrogging the Industrial Age Delivery System, we keep it and continue to deliver learning in a mass production way.....*thus pretending not to know.....*

Baby/Bathwater Metaphor

Quite some time ago we were conducting a workshop with a group of about eighty teachers and a few administrators. We of course were pontificating/lecturing/scolding/harping on the need for education to change, to modernize, to move into the Information Age. Well, that's what "consultants" are supposed to do . . . right?

As we listed the bureaucratic practices that needed to go if our profession was indeed going to act professionally, a teacher raised her hand and warned us, "We need to make sure that we don't throw the baby out with the bathwater." We had heard that one before, and immediately identified the teacher as a "resister." Our usual response to the baby/bathwater warning was to acknowledge the resister with a "yes, that's very true" and then quickly move on, attempting to influence those who were "open to change." But for some reason, on this occasion the baby/bathwater comment jumped out at us disguised as a "teachable moment."

We'll shorten the story, leave out the details, and simply say that on the spot we challenged the group to define "baby" and "bathwater" in regard to educational policies, practices, and structures. The group came alive and over the next thirty minutes we created the following . . . and have used it ever since.

"Don't Throw the Baby Out With the Bathwater!"
Ah, yes! But the essential question is:
So what's "baby" and what's "bathwater?"

BABY	BATHWATER
Those practices that have their roots in:	*Those practices and strategies that are based on:*
Research	Tradition
Accepted Theory	Norms
Expert Opinion	Convenience
Successful Experineces	Habit

What followed after creating and agreeing on the above definitions was to begin the creation of a list of babies and bathwater. The group rather quickly realized that:

> *You don't throw bathwater out just because it's bathwater!*
> *You throw bathwater out <u>when you have better bathwater</u>!*

You catch the subtleties of the baby/bathwater metaphor if you grew up on a Lakota reservation and are the fifth kid in a family of ten who took baths . . . when you did take baths . . . in a galvanized washtub with water heated on a wood burning stove. Been there, done that! (For the curious, the second batch of warm water is usually at about the right temperature somewhere between the third and fifth bather.)

<u>THE</u> Professional Question

In Chapter 3 we briefly explained THE question that moves us from bureaucrat to professional. The question, if even asked, is asked after the learner outcomes have been identified as part of the Strategic Design process. 'Tis a simple, subtle, and profession-changing question:

"How is this learner outcome best learned?"
(Please memorize . . . and never forget.)

Typically, the question educators ask after the learner outcome is determined is,

"How should/do/will we teach this?"

The focus is on the teacher and teaching. And, in all fairness, if you have experienced a bureaucratic educational system for all of your life, that is the natural and obvious question to ask. But if you are a professional, your initial thinking and decisions are client focused, focused first on the learner and learning rather than the teacher and teaching. So the question is not, "Is this a good teaching method?" but, "Is this a good learning method for the specific learning identified by our learner outcome?"

It is pertinent to note that asking THE question automatically makes the pure cyber school unacceptable. Although the computer and the Internet provide a powerful learning alternative, no professional educator would suggest that it is the best process for teaching the more qualitative learner outcomes that require face-to-face interaction with a professional learning facilitator and other learners.

We placed this brief explanation of "THE Question" here so that our following *Babies* can be viewed as a menu of options for the professional who is concerned with both the learner and learning, as well as the best research-based options available for this specific learning experience.

Our Assumptions

We are going to make some assumptions as we explain what we believe to be our ten most important *Babies* . . . those things we know about learners and learning that we don't want to lose, those things we don't want to throw out with the bathwater.

Assumption one:
Many of the *Babies* are so obvious and so universally understood that they don't require elaboration. You know much of this already. You learned about these *Babies* from your own learning experiences, from your experience as a parent, and/or your experiences as a teacher, a supervisor, or a leader. You will recognize those *Babies* when you see them.

Assumption two:
Inevitable is a book about restructuring and transforming education and not a book about learning theory. This chapter, *"About Learning: The Baby and the Bathwater,"* is intended to alleviate the concern that the **MCL** vision might force educators to stop using techniques and strategies that we know work for the good of learners. Should you desire to learn more about any one of our keepers, our *Babies*, you will find excellent books on any of these topics available from a number of organizations, including the Association for Supervision and Curriculum Development (ASCD) and Solution Tree.

Our Top Ten Babies

In the remainder of this chapter, we will define the *Babies*. . . .principles of learning from the research; those principles that help us to understand how human beings learn and the conditions under which human beings learn best.
But first, two "Rules of Thumb."

☑ One, if the process or structure perpetuates the Industrial Age assembly line delivery of instruction, it is BATHWATER — and has to go!

☑ Two, if the process or structure promotes and facilitates meeting the learning needs of individual students, it is BABY — it stays.

Our *Top Ten Babies* are not rocket science. That's the insidious part. We all *know* these things. Yet, our behaviors do not support them. We *pretend not to know* that:

1. *Learning rates vary and prior knowledge is significant to learning new knowledge.*
2. *Motivation spikes with learner interest.*
3. *Learning styles differ and intelligence is multi-dimensional.*
4. *Success breeds success and influences esteem, attitude, and motivation.*
5. *Mistakes are inherent in the learning process and specific feedback enhances learning.*
6. *Requisite complex reasoning skills can be taught/learned.*
7. *Real world contexts/problems enhance learning.*
8. *Learning is social.*
9. *Technology as teacher.*
10. *Schools/teachers control the conditions for learner success.*

Motivation Triggers

Our first four *Babies* all have to do with motivation . . . and they all deal with moving from extrinsic motivation to intrinsic motivation. From rewards and punishments as motivators, to support and creating motivating conditions. From control theory and practice, to support theory and practice. We believe that motivation is key to nearly everything. When motivation doesn't come from the inside, we attempt to create it from the outside. Sometimes extrinsic motivation works, most of the time it doesn't.

Let's cut to the chase . . .

> *Without intrinsic motivation to learn,*
> *we will forever be forced to force-feed learning.*

And that's why our top four *Babies* have to do in large part with creating the conditions that support intrinsic motivation. The following matrix summarizing Edward Deci's great book titled *Why We Do What We Do* draws sharp comparisons between controlling through extrinsic motivators and supporting through intrinsic motivators. We realize that you know much of what is on this comparison matrix . . . the point of putting it in front of us in this format is to succinctly show that Industrial Age, assembly line instructional delivery requires and sometimes forces extrinsic motivators . . . while **MCL**, from the start, is designed to create the conditions for intrinsic motivators.

Our strong belief: Teachers are intelligent, capable, and caring people who would love to have all intrinsically motivated learners who would achieve and achieve . . . but they work in an outdated, ingrained group-paced system that makes it ~~nearly~~ impossible to take advantage of our natural motivation to learn.

	CONTROL THEORY	**SUPPORT THEORY**
THE ULTIMATE GOAL	The Will to Learn	The Will to Learn
THE ESSENTIAL QUESTION	How do I motivate my students? My own children? My staff?	How do I set up the conditions so that my students, my own children, or my staff will be self-motivated?
THE MOTIVATORS	Control Theory uses: -rewards -punishments	Support Theory uses: -choice -challenge -competence
THE BEHAVIORAL GOAL	To "motivate" (manipulate) people to do what we want	To "motivate" (support) people in achieving their goal
THE RESULTING FRAME OF MIND	Which results in defiance or compliance	Which results in a general sense of well-being
THE UNDERLYING EMOTIONS	Which cultivates alienation	Which cultivates creativity, independence, self-actualization
THE LONG-TERM BEHAVIOR	Which UNDERMINES the original goal (the person does not choose to engage in the activity / task independent of the rewards or punishments)	Which SUSTAINS the original goal (the person is self-motivated to engage in the task / activity for the joy... sense of well-being)

Baby #1: *Learning rates vary and prior knowledge is significant to learning new knowledge.*

That learners learn at different rates is one of those *Babies* that does not need elaboration. Research has proven this to be true as have our personal experiences.

That "prior knowledge is significant to learning new knowledge" might not be quite so obvious . . . but we have all experienced it. Madeline Hunter, one of our heroines, taught us that THE most important factor in determining if the learner will grasp what we are attempting to teach them is: "Does the learner have the prerequisite learnings?" For example (and math examples always seem to be more easily understood), multiplication is a shortcut for addition and division is a short-cut for subtraction, and so it is best that learners know addition and subtraction before expecting them to learn, and understand, multiplication and division.

To go a bit further with the math examples, our assembly line schools allow only so much time to complete Algebra I. Those that master Algebra I and are able to deal successfully with quadratic equations get an "A" and are ready to go on to Algebra II. Those who don't master quadratic equations, but hand in all of their assignments and get passing grades on tests, might get a "B-." Which student has mastered Algebra I and has the "prerequisite learnings" that will lead to success in Algebra II?

MASS CUSTOMIZED LEARNING (**MCL**), on the other hand, makes learning the constant and time the variable. When the learner masters Algebra I and can demonstrate that learning by solving quadratic equations, he/she will have the demonstration of that learning made part of his/her electronic portfolio and go on to Algebra II with the foundation required to be successful with his/her Algebra II learner outcomes. A BIG intrinsic motivator is triggered when a learner knows that he/she will be challenged with a higher level task, but has come to trust that the system has provided him/her with the requisite learning to meet the challenge.

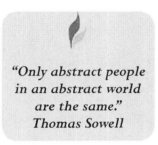

"Only abstract people in an abstract world are the same."
Thomas Sowell

Baby #2: *Motivation spikes with learner interest.*

Our interests, those things that excite us and make us want to learn, are most likely even more varied than our learning rates. Today's world requires that everyone be lifelong learners (LLLs) and we adults typically choose what and how we will learn the things that we need to know to live successful and meaningful lives. Most of us have experienced the intrinsic motivation that comes with the freedom to choose what we will learn. Learning that which is both interesting and meaningful spikes our motivation to learn . . . be that about career development, about becoming expert at something, or about a fun hobby.

Typically, 13-year-olds don't get to learn things that are of interest, or to learn basic skills and concepts via content that is of interest. The assembly line, group-paced school structure makes it difficult if not impossible for even the best teacher to meet the unique interests of individual learners.

Excuse the math examples, but how many different ways can we teach the basic skill of long division? One way is through a math text that may have one or two examples of how the skill will be used in real life. But it could also be learned by keeping a weekly record of the pass completion percentages of Spencer's five favorite NFL quarterbacks. Lori could learn to write a business plan by working through a classic case study in which the type of business is already determined. Or she might write a business plan for the music business she dreams of creating which is the top interest for her today as she thinks of future careers. Lincoln might have to be bribed or threatened to learn geometry, but tie that learning to architecture and you will have a motivated kid who would be excited about lines, angles, and forms.

MCL makes aligning learning with learner interest relatively simple. Intrinsic motivation runs on learner interest. LLL is fueled by intrinsic motivation. There may always be a need to learn something that is not of interest, but they should be few and far between. Content, and therefore interest, should be the variable; being able to demonstrate the required skill or concept should be the constant.

Reward and/or punishment are to extrinsic motivation

as

Interest and relevance are to intrinsic motivation.
MCL provides the option.

Baby #3: *Learning styles differ and intelligence is multi-dimensional.*

Some of the smartest and most successful people we know were not very good students. And some of the most successful people we know were very good students. There are many ways to be intelligent and many ways to find success with the intelligences that we possess. Educators, and our society as a whole, seem to equate intelligence with scholastic aptitude, although Howard Gardner made "multiple intelligences" part of the vocabulary years back. Gardner told us about six ways to be intelligent. Recently William Spady identified twenty-five ways of being intelligent, and Daniel Pink, in *A Whole New Mind*, asserts that the future belongs to a very different kind of person with a very different kind of mind.....all understandable and believable. The first ... and we think the recent ... IQ tests were/are designed to identify those most likely to be successful as.... well.....university students. *But life is about <u>more than</u> being good university students.*

85

So what? What to make of this? For example, the lecture method is one used in many secondary classrooms. **MCL** asks the question, "How is this learner outcome best learned?" Extended, the question might be " How is this learner outcome best learned by this specific learner?" You might learn the outcome best by listening to a well-designed lecture. I might learn it best if I discussed it with a mentor and was able to ask questions. Others

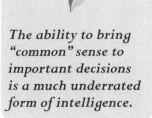

The ability to bring "common" sense to important decisions is a much underrated form of intelligence.

may learn it best by designing and creating something. Some learn best in small groups, hence the success of cooperative learning. The learning style should fit the learner, and the learner outcome can be demonstrated in different ways. Bottom line . . . don't give up on the learner just because he/she is not articulate or not deemed intelligent when only scholastic aptitude is the determiner of intelligence. We need to make learning style and the application of differing intelligences the variable, and the demonstration of the learner outcomes the constant. The ability to bring "common sense" to important decisions is a much underrated form of intelligence.

A Little Story (cjs): I was a basketball coach the first three years of my teaching career. We had good kids, good teams, insisted on team efforts and sportsmanship, won a state championship. Got to know kids in a different setting. Some of my fondest educator memories. Although many of our best players were also very good students, one of our all-staters spent most of his school hours in remedial classes. But at 3:15, when you tossed him a basketball, his IQ immediately hit 135. I learned to watch some of the moves he made with the ball that consistently got him points, designed drills to teach others those moves, and our team continually improved as a result. Not only a successful basketball player, he is now living a very successful post-basketball life. He knew his strengths and found a career that fit his talents and passion.

Coaching basketball also helped me with another learning that I believe we need to apply to our learners and our instructional delivery systems. And you will see that **MCL** makes the wholesale application of my learning possible.

I watched eighth and ninth grade boys who were excellent players, bound to be stars. And of course I watched clumsy, beanpole kids whom I was tempted to influence to quit the sport and save their embarrassment. You probably already know where this story is going. When these same groups of kids were in their varsity years, their rankings had changed considerably. The beanpole suddenly became coordinated and could hit the basket, and the sure hit star, although a contributing member of the team was not a starter. True story . . . at the beginning of the basketball season, one boy (wish I could use names) was at the tail end of our list of 15 boys who would make the varsity. Truth be known, he probably made the team because we knew that his mother was terminally ill with cancer and we thought that he would need the emotional support. The assumption that the fifteenth kid on the varsity will probably not win or lose you any games anyway might have influenced our thinking.

The short ending of the story. The fifteenth kid, then a junior, got into his first game about a third of the way through the season. We were playing a team that we should have dominated and we were only up by 6 midway through the second quarter. In a move meant to shock our starters, we put "fifteenth" into the game. He scored 6 before half, another 10 in the second half, started the next game, was unanimous all-state on our championship team as a senior, and scored 48 in his first game as a college freshman.

So what does this have to do with **MCL**? You might think that we were simply poor judges of basketball talent, but we were not. Fifteenth was fifteenth then. But he matured quickly, got bigger, and put it all together in his junior year. Fifteenth's growth as a basketball player became obvious to us . . . and to everyone. It was physical, it could be seen, there was a way of keeping score, he was scoring points, he was getting rebounds, and our team was winning.

We believe that the same growth spurts happen with the intellect as well as the physical. We have personally experienced it. The assembly line school system doesn't recognize when "fifteenth" is ready to shine, to become a star. Second graders are put into reading groups. Fifteenth is in the blackbird reading group. He is labeled by the system as a blackbird group kid and is again a blackbird in grade three. He begins to see himself as a blackbird and begins living up to his own expectations and the blackbird expectations of the system. **MCL** allows for spurts, for increased motivation, for changing expectations of self and others, for achievement gains that would never have been expected.

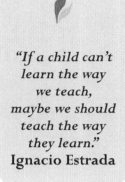

"If a child can't learn the way we teach, maybe we should teach the way they learn."
Ignacio Estrada

Baby #4: *Success breeds success and influences esteem, attitude, and motivation.*

We *know* that success breeds success; failure breeds failure. Yet we are still baffled by and hugely irritated with a ninth grader who has failed math for 9 years and either totally disrupts our Applied Algebra class or spends the entire class with his head on the desk. Martin Covington, in <u>The Will To Learn</u>, describes such a student – with his head on his desk as actually <u>very motivated</u>. Huh?

He explains one is either driven to succeed, anticipating hope and pride; or driven to avoid failure, anticipating shame and humiliation. Drive Theory is one aspect of current research on the nature of motivation.

A Little Story (bmcg): *A middle school teacher in one of my sessions told me this story, which I have recounted numerous times. She had one of those students Covington describes: head on his desk the entire class period. After weeks of ignoring his behavior, she resolves one morning while dressing for school that she is no longer going to tolerate such behavior. In fact, she was working herself into a dither which continued on the drive to school and into the assistant principal's office to warn him that come Period 3, he could expect this student in his office. I can hear her rant now!*

Period 3 arrives and again, his head is down! Just as she is about to kick his adolescent butt (her words!) out of class, a little voice (you know, that teacher voice…that teacher-angel voice OR that teacher-devil voice) suggests she try a strategy described recently by a colleague. And so she does. After class, she takes him aside and says she needs him to pay attention and participate, which means head up and hand up when a question is asked. The deal was to raise his right hand if he knew the answer and his left if he didn't. She promised she would never call on him if his left hand is raised. Deal? Well, of course, his response was typical of an adolescent: surly! She was doubtful it would work and was prepared to institute her initial strategy: send him to the office!

The next day, Period 3. Class begins. His head is up. She teaches, asks a question of the class. Hands go up. His hand goes up. Wow! It is his left hand; she double checks lest she make a huge error! Left hand. She walks toward him; makes eye contact; and moves to another student for the answer. This goes on for weeks, she says. Until one day, she notices his right hand is up. She calls on him. Correct answer! He continues to participant the rest of the year. Success!

What a perfect example of Covington's explanation of Drive Theory! This middle school student WAS highly motivated. You see, he would rather be seen as being <u>lazy</u> and suffering the fallout of being tagged with this moniker — not a comfortable place to be, but waaaaay better than being seen as someone who failed. Lazy or failure? Hmm….the choice was clear to him: *highly motivated to avoid failure.*

There are countless research studies and resources for our #4 Baby. Our favorites include:

> Daniel Pink, <u>*Drive*</u>
> Martin Covington, <u>*The Will To Learn*</u>
> Mihaly Csikszentmhayi, <u>*Flow*</u>
> Edward Deci, <u>*Why We Do What We Do*</u>

Baby #5: *Mistakes are inherent in the learning process and specific feedback enhances learning.*

Over the past ten years or so we have frequently heard and read . . . from authorities . . . that we learn more from our failures than from our successes. Our parents and our teachers of long ago didn't appear to subscribe to this position. Failure brought forth lectures from parents and was identified in red by teachers.

But these are different times. The world is moving much faster. In the leadership and business books that we read we have learned that the successful innovative organizations fail about 80% of the time. But they quickly learn when a new strategy or technique is not working and are fast to abandon it, learn from it, and move on to the next risk taking experiment.

The reason that these failing organizations are very successful is that when they are right, that 20% of the time, they make money big time and milk it for all it's worth for as long as it continues to work for them. They are not right more often than the others but, not fearing failure, they try more "good" ideas and therefore have more successes and consequently more profit than the others. (Read that sentence again . . . it really does make sense.)

It is interesting to watch a typical digital native age ten or so manipulate a computer or an online game. *They never read instructions. Instead they just start!* If it was a good start they make the next intuitive move. If it's not a good start they hit the back button and try again. In either case, they learn what works and what doesn't work and quickly move on. At the end of their experience, they have not only learned how to work that specific program or a game, but they have learned a deeper reality of interactive technology. They will be even more intuitive the next time they meet a new program or a new game. They now know more about how program and game designers think. They are continuously and quickly learning, continuously improving, and are not afraid to make mistakes.

We digital immigrants usually don't think that way. A mistake is a mistake, darn it; an error is an error, darn it! Mistakes, errors, and failures are to be avoided. Didn't the turtle actually win that race? Haven't we heard about people actually being fired because they took a risk that didn't pan out?

But failure only teaches when we understand, or think we understand, why we might have failed. Ken Blanchard of *One Minute Manager* fame says, "Feedback is the breakfast of champions!" Feedback is best and most powerful when it is specific rather than general, provided in the here-and-now, modeled by a learning coach, and when it provides the learner the opportunity for a quick second try. When learning is customized, feedback can be built into the instructional design. Following the rules for powerful personal feedback is much more problematic in classrooms of one teacher and twenty-five learners.

Baby #6: *Requisite complex reasoning skills can be taught / learned.*

We tend to <u>teach</u> content at a literal level; now, content can still be engaging, but it is still at the literal comprehension level. Then, we give an assignment that requires kids to use complex reasoning processes with that knowledge, yet we seldom explicitly and directly teach the reasoning processes (e.g., deductive reasoning, abstract reasoning, problem solving reasoning, analyzing perspectives reasoning, constructing support reasoning, etc.) that are required to be successful at these assignments/activities . . . as well as to be successful in real life. These are all skills which have steps to them and which can and need to be taught.

> *The difference between school and life?*
> *In school,*
> *you're taught a lesson and given a test.*
> *In life,*
> *you're given a test that teaches you a lesson.*
> **Tom Bodett**

The insidious part of this is that when we teach literal content and then require kids to apply it with a reasoning process – without teaching the reasoning process – the resulting work of the learners is some semblance of the "bell curve" - some of the work is outstanding, most is okay, and some is very bad. Unfortunately, teachers draw the conclusions: "see some kids are smart and others are not so smart . . . and that's just the way it is." When – what really happened was – the kids who did well walked in the door knowing how to do deductive reasoning etc.; while those who did poorly – well . . . the teacher did not teach them how to do the requisite reasoning process. We would never require kids to do the skill of two-digit multiplication if we never taught it to them. Yet, we require kids all the time to do complex reasoning processes that we have never explicitly and directly taught them. Another irony for us is that when we look at items on a state test . . where for many questions, the content is actually given . . . the question is asking kids to see a pattern (abstract reasoning), make a prediction (deductive reasoning), take a stand and support it (constructing support reasoning), and so on. Again, poor tests scores give evidence to us that we don't teach these complex reasoning skills.

> *"If it's important, it should be intentional."*
> **Stephen Covey**

91

Baby #7: *Real world context / problems enhance learning.*

Relevance is a key to learner motivation. Motivation is key to engagement, learning, and achievement. Real-life, concrete problems provide that relevance for learners. Most of us will remember the difference between doing a page of thirty multiplication problems with two or three digits in the multiplier, and a good story problem that asked us to find the number of square feet in a football field and calculate the cost of installing new turf at a price of $1.25 per square foot. "Ohhhh, so that's why we need to do multiplication with three digits in the multiplier."

The story of Jackie Robinson becoming the first black player in major league baseball brings the reality of racism to the fifth grader who is a Dodger fan. He learns of the courage, the pain, and the eventual joy of Robinson's experiences. Empathy for those real people who were discriminated against moves the learner from "understanding" racism to making commitments to not be racist. Abstract discussions of the cause and history of racism, without a real world emotional tie, leave the concept of racism itself an abstraction that may or may not be remembered, understood, or applied by the learner.

Field trips (virtual or actual) are fun for learners of all ages because they help abstract concepts discussed in readings and classrooms come alive. If schools are for the purpose of getting learners ready for life, for "empowering all learners to succeed in a rapidly changing world," then school and real life have to meet in learning activities that take place in a real world context.

Some fear that learning in real life contexts leads to a lack of intellectual rigor, and that involving learners in a community project is not an efficient use of time. To those with these fears, we would suggest that if "real life" doesn't have rigor, then what does . . . "life" is as rigorous as our world will get! (*You might want to give that last sentence a second read . . . we did!*) And for those who are concerned about learning time, there is much to be said for "less is more," that in-depth learning of fewer concepts is ultimately more helpful to the learner that "covering" great amounts of content.

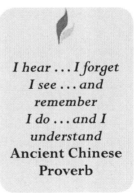

*I hear . . . I forget
I see . . . and
remember
I do . . . and I
understand*
**Ancient Chinese
Proverb**

Baby #8: *Learning is social.*

This sounds trite, but it is a HUGE *Baby*: Learning is all about relationships . . . this is a deal breaker! It reminds us that leaders must first and foremost be authentic individuals and be viewed as such. (Much more about leadership in Chapter 10, *Total Leaders*.) A student needs to know AND FEEL that the learning facilitator AUTHENTICALLY cares. You can't fudge this one. Kids can smell a phony a mile away!

Some adults very naturally love kids . . . they should be teachers. Some adults quite naturally don't love kids . . . they should not be teachers. Loving one's field of study and not particularly caring for kids might work for teachers, but it won't trip the motivation wire for most learners. Expect the need for rewards and/or punishment to be necessary. The best fit, and what should be expected to be the only acceptable fit, is when the teacher loves both his/her content and learners. Teachers who relate to young learners have a natural tendency to see learning from the learner's perspective. They are more apt to concern themselves with learning styles and arenas of interest, more apt to trip the learner's intrinsic motivation wire.

The Net Generation is heavily into social networks as evidenced by the popularity of *Twitter, MySpace, Facebook*, etc. Educators should tie the strong desire of today's youth to network with the powerful research regarding cooperative learning. We have to embrace that research and accompanying teaching techniques. We must be careful to avoid being stuck in the Industrial Age thinking that it is cheating to work collaboratively.

On a side note, we (McGarvey and Schwahn) relearn nearly monthly that learning is not really internalized until we have taught it to someone else. And it seems that when we struggle with helping someone else to learn, we learn it at an even deeper level. We are reminded of the cross-age peer grouping studies of about 20 years ago where the findings clearly indicated that the younger learner learned more from his slightly older partner than did the learners in the control group. The surprise finding, however, was that the older student, the peer teacher, gained even more than did the younger partner.

More on relationships . . . this part in the form of an observation.

An Observation (bmcg): As a guidance counselor in a middle school, I learned very quickly that the same kids behaved differently in different classrooms. I could easily see that the constant was the learner, the variable the teacher. What made the difference? It was all about the teacher's attitude toward the learner. When the teacher communicated — in many explicit and implicit ways — that they authentically cared

> about the learner, the learner . . . well . . . learned and behaved; they were engaged. And vice versa. And it was not that the engaging teachers were "pushovers." In many cases, these were very tough teachers — with high expectations — but they communicated over and over again that they knew their content, could teach it, believed the kid could learn it, and had a way of letting the learner know that "I exist so you will be successful." The kids knew it, and bought into it!

Baby #9: *Technology as teacher.*

Gaming and online learning are among the fastest growing and most lucrative markets today. And games and online learning are becoming increasingly more sophisticated as they gain in popularity. Virtual reality is coming . . . we "ain't seen nothin' yet!" But, already now as we write about **MCL**, gaming and online learning have made their mark. We don't have to wait. Online learning opportunities on any topic seem to exist everywhere. Bing or Google what you want to learn about and the teacher will be there. The educators with whom we have worked over the past few years estimate that, at a minimum, 50% of what we now want learners to learn could be taught via technology.

Educators need to avoid the natural tendency to become defensive about "technology as teacher." Teachers will never be replaced. When necessary but somewhat mundane knowledge, concepts, and skills can be taught as well or better by a computer, THEY SHOULD BE. Anytime we can effectively move learning to the computer, we leave the "professional" teacher more time to teach the more important learner outcomes that require interaction, demonstration, and coaching. We firmly believe that **MCL** will professionalize education. Our Industrial Age school systems tend to be mirrors of industries. (Just realized that the last sentence is internally redundant.)

Baby #10: *Schools / teachers control the conditions for learner success.*

It's easy to place blame when it comes to unsuccessful learners, to low achievement levels, to discipline problems, to dropout rates, etc. And in reality, whether it's helpful or not to place blame, there are many out there who are guilty. There *are* many other forces in our society that are not aligned with the need to create a context for student success. But as psychologist after psychologist has taught us, "If we place blame for our lack of success with particular learners, we give away our power to solve a problem that obviously impacts us."

When that learner walks in our door, his/her learning is *our* problem and *our* opportunity. Owning that reality empowers us to create the conditions for learner success. Blaming parents, the entertainment industry, our permissive anything-goes contemporary culture, or an economy that requires both parents to work, depowers us. Empowered people are in control of the variables they perceive important to their success. They are ready to "get at it." Depowered people require that others first do their job so that they can do theirs . . . good luck with that!

A Little Story (bmcg): A couple of years ago, I worked with the Kennedy Middle School staff in El Centro, CA., a community in the southernmost part of the state. As I drove to the school on the morning of the workshop, a huge wave of discouragement and futility came over me. The poverty in this neighborhood was overwhelming. I could identify 50 reasons why students would be unsuccessful in this school — without even going into the school! The teachers, the poor teachers, must be discouraged, exhausted, negative, and probably more than cynical. And...now, I show up - to talk with them about research-based strategies. Whoopie! I thought, with justified sarcasm, this was going to be a great day!

Well, shame on me! The minute I entered the school, it was like an oasis. I could feel the empowered culture. (It is easy for those of us who work with school staffs to "see" and "feel" culture immediately....it is like a 6th sense.) Evidence of success was everywhere....from test scores....to attendance rates.....to dramatic decreases in all negatives (dropout rate, vandalism, etc.). When I quizzed Suzanne Smith, the principal, on why they were achieving such success, she pointed to the teachers and went on to sing their praises. When I asked teachers why they were so successful, they pointed to the principal. Okay...mutual respect. A good thing.

Midway through the day, I stopped my teaching. I observed that they were so busy doing what they were doing that they couldn't articulate what it is that contributed to their success. I suggested that they ask someone from a nearby university — someone skilled in capturing a "portrait" of a school - to visit for a couple of weeks. How valuable to them and others it would be to identify their ingredients for success.

> At this point, a young teacher, who had only been teaching for 2 years, (I call these young teachers "puppies") raised his hand and said, "I'm not sure if this has anything to do with it, but what I've noticed is that if we have data that shows our students are not being successful, <u>we take it personally!</u>" I wanted to hug him! He had just identified one of major characteristics of an empowered staff......a staff with a very strong sense of efficacy; in other words, they <u>believe</u> that they have the ability to help students be successful. They know it won't be easy; but they KNOW they can teach and they KNOW these kids can learn!

With our assembly line school systems, where students are grouped by age and placed in a math or English class, the question that we might ask ourselves as each learner walks through *our* door might be, "Will Bob/Betty be ready for solving equations that contain two unknowns today, and if not, what might happen for him/her today?" "Will Bob/Betty be ready to begin to create an outline for an essay he/she will write today, and if not, what might happen for him/her today?" These questions are system-centered questions. The bureaucratic system is the constant, and learner readiness is the variable.

In contrast, the question asked when Bob and Betty walk through the **MCL** school door is a learner-centered question, "What is Bob/Betty ready for today?"

About the Bathwater

You will recall from earlier in the chapter that we don't throw bathwater out just because it is bathwater. We only throw the bathwater out when there is better, cleaner, more effective bathwater available. So what are our bathwaters that we must retain until we get better bathwaters? In other words, what are school systems now doing that do not add value to, and in many cases actually detract from, the learning process.

Eight of these bathwaters make up the listing of *Weight Bearing Walls* that you will learn about in Chapter 8. That listing includes:

Grade Levels
> *that will be replaced by continuous learning.*

Students Permanently Assigned to Specific Classrooms
> *that will be replaced by temporary groupings dependent on the learning needs of particular learners at that particular time.*

Class Periods/Bell Schedules

> *that will be replaced by time frames for learning based upon the nature of the learner outcome.*

Courses/Curriculum

> *that will be replaced by learner outcomes and Information Age communication technology.*

Textbooks

> *that will be replaced by the nearly unlimited information available on the web.*

Paper and Pencil Records

> *that will be replaced by computers and data storage devices.*

ABC Grading

> *that will be replaced by demonstrations of learning outcomes and electronic learner portfolios.*

Report Cards

> *that will be replaced by online, real-time access to each learner's records of achievement by only those who have been identified as having "a need to know."*

Learning Happens in School

> *that will be replaced by: the community IS the Learning Community.*

Nine-Month School Year

> *that will be replaced by "learning by anyone, from anywhere, at any time."*

We will expect that each of you will have "babies" and "bathwaters" of your own. Start your own list. Have some fun. We know school districts that keep a running list of babies and bathwaters. Look for them. They are everywhere!

Chapter 5
Takeaways:

If we meet the needs of the learner regarding learning level, learning style, and learning interest, we can expect intrinsically motivated learners. If we do not meet these learner needs, we will be forced to continue to rely on the extrinsic motivators – rewards and punishments.

MCL retains "best practices" and acts on all our best research regarding learners and learning.

MCL provides a context in which educators are allowed, encouraged, and supported in their commitment to be true professionals, and to be part of a larger profession.

Chapter 6
MCL: The Vision (Detailed)

"Your successful past will block your visions of the future."

Joel Barker

Chapter 6 Intent

**To paint a concrete vision of a doable instructional
delivery system
that meets the daily learning needs of every learner.
To show that MASS CUSTOMIZED LEARNING can be done,
and to concretely and systematically describe
one/a way to do it.**

In Chapter 3 we identified and described the three direction-setting components
of a comprehensive Strategic Design:

First, organizational direction should be based on a clear moral foundation . . .
usually taking the form of the identification of and commitment to a set
of inspirational core values.

Second, and most basic, effective organizations identify and communicate their
mission, their purpose for being. For school systems, this mission/pur-
pose typically speaks to preparing learners for a successful life in a rapidly changing world.

Third, and this step is unique to educational organizations, effective school systems identify the learner outcomes that will ensure that graduates are
prepared for the challenges and opportunities that our "rapidly changing world" will present.

These three elements of Strategic Design are about *direction*, about goals if
you would, about the "what" of organizations.

While organizational vision is also a clear and critical direction setter, it is
not about "what," but about "how." Vision is about clearly and concretely identifying what the organization will look like, feel like, and be like when all three
direction-setting commitments are being realized.

Vision Defined

The labels mission and vision are sometimes thought to be synonyms. They are
not. Mission is about purpose, what the organization will accomplish. Vision is
about structures, policies, and practices, what the organization itself will be. If

this is what we want to accomplish (mission), then this is how we will look when doing it (vision). Chapter 6 will provide a number of examples of vision statements that will help to clarify and extend the following definition:

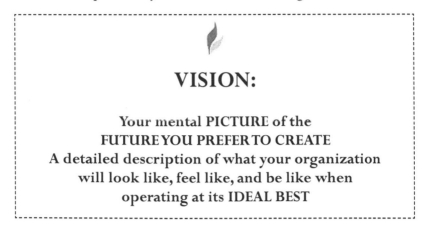

VISION:

Your mental PICTURE of the
FUTURE YOU PREFER TO CREATE
A detailed description of what your organization
will look like, feel like, and be like when
operating at its IDEAL BEST

Visions, to be powerful, must run well ahead of the organization's present capacity to do them. Visions "pull" rather than "push" people, teams, and organizations toward an exciting and ideal future. Visionary leaders take people beyond where they would have gone without them. The best example of a vision statement doing just that, all of that . . . and more, was John F. Kennedy's 1962 "Man on the Moon" vision statement . . . "This nation should dedicate itself to achieving the goal, before this decade is out, of landing a man on the moon and returning him safely to earth." At that time NASA leaders estimated that they knew about 15% of what they needed to know to get there. But, we knew that it was right. When we think "vision," we think "challenge, excitement, discovery, innovation, ideal, right thing to do, and worth it all."

> *Visionary leaders take people beyond where they would have gone without them.*

Psychologists and leadership gurus also advise that vision statements are also more powerful if written in present rather than future tense. So the vision statements that follow throughout Chapter 6 are written as though they are already happening. Stating the ideal in present tense seems to create a sense of excitement, doability, and commitment.

Today's leaders are future-focused visionaries. Today it is expected that leaders know and "*do the right thing*" . . . and that managers "*do the thing right*." Both leadership and management are important and critical roles, but they are different. Rapid change requires future-focused visionaries who keep their eyes on the horizon. Managers manage the vision, do the heavy lifting, make tough calls, and make things happen. (More about leadership in Chapter 10, "*Total Leaders*," and yet more about leadership in Schwahn and Spady's *Total Leaders 2.0*. and *Learning Communities 2.0* written for the American Association of School Administrators.)

From Schools to Learning Communities

The MASS CUSTOMIZED LEARNING vision is bold, it is transformational and, beyond that, it is also:

☑ Describable: clear, concrete, and easily communicated

☑ Desirable: an ideal future that excites and enthuses

☑ Doable: but not without risking and heroic efforts

☑ Directing: for the individual and the organization

☑ Detailed: so that everyone knows how it impacts them

Words matter! Think "School District and Schools." Now think "Learning Community and Learning Centers." Think "students." Then think "learners." Think "classes and courses." Now think "learner outcomes and learning opportunities." When working with groups we sometimes ask participants to close their eyes while we slowly say these pairs of words. Participants are amazed at how differently their mind images the first and second word. They quickly realize that the second word(s) in each set allows for visualizing multiple alternatives.

When we think "Learning Communities" it's quite easy to visualize economics and budgeting being taught in the conference room of First National by bank officers; easy to see a fifteen-year-old girl or boy being mentored by the owner of a landscaping company; easy to see a social science group planning, budgeting, preparing, and serving a meal to the homeless. All of these activities are not simply good experiences, but experiences that allow learners to demonstrate predetermined learner outcomes that fit back into the "Empowering all learners to be successful in a rapidly changing world" mission and accompanying Spheres of Living.

When we say schools, it's quite easy to visualize long hallways, classrooms on each side, rows of desks, teachers lecturing, students slouched in their seats, bells ringing, and suddenly energized teenagers as they happily exit Central High. (Spady and Schwahn's *Learning Communities 2.0* mentioned above provides a detailed and contrasting description of a Learning Community and a School District.)

Meaningful change begins with a bold vision of the possible.
A new vocabulary is required if people are to open their minds to real change.
The new vocabulary must be introduced, modeled, and encouraged by leaders.

Planning for Change.....or Not

You have probably heard the old truism, "If you always do what you've always done you'll always get what you've always gotten." Now, your humble authors have been around the block. This ain't our first rodeo! (Yea, we know better, but "ain't" just seems to fit here.) And what we see in case after case and place after place, whenever educators talk of strategic planning and the need for change, they never think about changing the organizational structure of schools. It isn't that they think about it and decide not to change the structure, it is that they don't even give it a thought. Schools WILL HAVE grade levels, students will be grouped according to age, we will teach them in groups, we will measure their achievement by grades, they will be moved through the system, and there will be a class rank.

The Strategic Design process described in Chapter 3 is strikingly different from any other strategic planning process we have encountered. And the difference begins with an assumption.

> We believe / assume that form follows function; that if we change the mission and learner outcomes of our school system to accommodate today's new demands, we will have to change the structure of the system to accommodate the new expectations.

Other planners and planning processes assume that our present outdated, graded, Industrial Age, assembly line structure is a "given." A given for all time.

Ours is a vertical planning process that begins at the top. The process is logical. There is a clear rationale for each step. We begin with a study of the future, identify our learner centered mission, derive learner outcomes based on the vision, create a curriculum based on those outcomes, determine how learners can best learn to demonstrate those outcomes, and then . . . <u>AND ONLY THEN</u>, we begin to consider how our system should be structured to deliver the instruction/learning opportunities.

Theirs is a horizontal planning process. Most frequently, groups are formed and assigned the task of setting goals for a specific part of the strategic plan. One group might be working on the mission statement, another on curriculum, another on instruction, another on technology, another on facilities, and so forth. Groups work simultaneously with little communication between them before they present their recommendations to the total group. How can they do this??? Won't the mission be a strong influence on curriculum, won't a new vision have a strong influence on facilities, etc.?

Well no, they won't! There was a silent, unconscious agreement made at the beginning of the planning process that there would be no significant changes made. They had agreed, albeit without talking about it, that only tinkering and cosmetic changes would be considered. Everything will basically remain the same so the facilities group knows what the vision group will propose; and the curriculum group knows that they are not expected to systematically relate the curriculum to the mission statement. The mission group knows that what they are actually doing is writing the slogan that will go on business cards and stationery.

'Tis hard to get to the future, to MASS CUSTOMIZED LEARNING with this type of planning process. And by the way, the people who give of their time to create these "no change expected" plans are good people, capable people, intelligent people. But they, and the strategic planning facilitator, have spent years – many years – in Industrial Age, assembly line schools to the point that they literally can't see any other way to do it. They don't ask the right questions. The "right" questions that are listed and described in Chapter 3.

Your organization is
perfectly designed to get
the results that you are getting.

A Mass Customized Learning Vision

The Sycamore Community School District Strategic Design planning group created the detailed vision statement that follows. (Sycamore is a rather typical school district in Illinois that serves about 4000 students. The vision statement is for real, mostly, altered only a bit to be more tightly aligned with **MCL**. You will learn as you study their vision, that the SCSD has a strong and capable leadership team.)

After studying the future conditions learners will encounter after graduation, and after clearly identifying the three direction-setting elements of the SD process (Core Values, Mission Statement, Learning Outcomes), the Sycamore planning group asked the question,

"What will our school system look like, feel like, and be like when we are effectively acting on our values, meeting our mission, and ensuring that all graduates are able to demonstrate our exit learner outcomes?"

For a vision statement to be powerful and direction setting, it must be stated in a concrete and rather comprehensive manner. So that the SD planning group could be organized around the critical components of their school system, we first identified the system elements that most impacted the learner and learning. The Sycamore group, with a bit of guidance from their humble facilitators, agreed on the following:

LEARNING	*From a student perspective*
CURRICULUM	*What we expect students to learn*
INSTRUCTION	*How we help students to learn*
ASSESSMENT	*How we measure student success and are held accountable*
TECHNOLOGY	*How we use technology to customize and increase learning*
STAKEHOLDERS	*How we involve all members of the community*
PERSONNEL	*Whom we employ as an ideal staff*
LEADERSHIP	*How we provide support at all levels*

Members of the SD planning group were familiar with the **MCL** vision, and the Board of Education and Leadership Team had made a tentative commitment to the **MCL** concept in advance of the planning session. For this visioning process, groups were formed around the eight vision components listed above. Members selected the group that best matched their expertise and interest. Groups created a first draft, presented their drafts to the total group, received feedback and modified their vision statements, and again presented them to the total group.

The order of the components of the vision statements is relevant. While most planning processes are organization oriented, **MCL** is learner focused. So we start with the learner experience, move to the components that directly impact learners, and then to the components that support the system. Please take your time and create an image in your mind about each of the vision components . . . open your mind to create a visual picture of each component.

Note: *Many of the following vision statements may cause you to say, "Yea, wouldn't that be nice, but there is no way that it can be done . . . get real, guys!" And that reaction is justified . . . justified IF you are thinking of doing them in today's Industrial Age schools. But we are proposing a modern structure for school systems that allows for and promotes* MASS CUSTOMIZED LEARNING.

Chapter 7, "Lori Does Her Learning Schedule," Chapter 8, "Weight Bearing Walls," and Chapter 9, "Ready for Rollout" describe how it can / will be done. (It is INEVITABLE, *you know.) So trust us, relax, be believers knowing that it can be done and that you will learn how to implement all of these vision statements, visions that you know are most consistent with learners, learning, and effective organizations.*

The following is a draft of the Sycamore School District's Visions for LEARNING, CURRICULUM, INSTRUCTION, ASSESSMENT, TECHNOLOGY, STAKEHOLDERS, PERSONNEL, and LEADERSHIP. We are reminded of Joel Barker's essential vision question:

"What seems impossible to do in your organization today, but if you could do it, it would fundamentally change the results?"

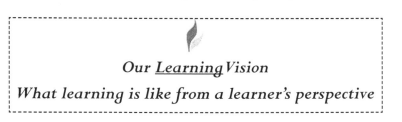

Our <u>Learning</u> Vision
What learning is like from a learner's perspective

I am very involved in the planning of my learning experiences. My learning coach from school and my parents get involved by helping me set my direction; but as I progress, I am becoming more responsible for designing and scheduling my own learning program.

Every day, I come to school and am met at my developmental learning level, I am challenged, I am usually very successful, and I leave school wanting to return tomorrow.

All Sycamore students are naturally highly motivated to learn because the learning experiences of each student are matched to his/her developmental learning level, his/her learning styles, strengths, and interests.

I learn in many ways -- about one-half of my learning is online, I take part in numerous seminars with other learners, I attend large group lectures, I read a lot, and I learn from mentors in our community.

Sycamore students believe that today's world requires lifelong learners, and teachers design learning activities to ensure that graduates leave the school system as self-directed, future-focused, lifelong learners. As I advance through my program, I increasingly become accountable for my own learning.

I have an electronic learner outcome portfolio that shows a complete record of my learning accomplishments. My parents, my learning coach, and my teachers (those with a need to know) have access to my portfolio.

Our world is becoming increasingly global and diverse, and Sycamore learners continuously learn to embrace diversity . . . diversity of cultures, religions, ethnicity, and ways of viewing the world.

All Sycamore students leave our school system with the opportunity to choose any future they desire . . . graduates are ready for college, for employment, and/or for creatively designing their own future.

Sycamore has become recognized as the place to visit to watch students and adults study, analyze, and debate cultural, religious, economic, and global issues.

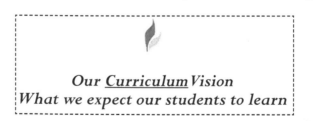

Our _Curriculum_ Vision
What we expect our students to learn

All curriculum is written in a "learner outcome" format and is directly aligned with Sycamore's mission and exit learner outcomes.

The Sycamore Strategic Design process identified the exit learning outcomes for all students. When students graduate from our system, they are able to demonstrate all exit learner outcomes .... which means that they have been "empowered to succeed in their world."

The curriculum for each level of learning and each department is also written in a student learner outcomes format that makes it clear what students must do/demonstrate to show mastery.

At all times, Sycamore learners know how what they are being asked/required to learn will impact their success after they leave school. All learning is related to life. All learning is viewed as relevant by the learner.

The learner outcomes for Sycamore focus on the whole child/learner; they ensure that each child/learner is prepared academically, socially, and emotionally. We are concerned with what our learners know, what they are able to do, and what kind of person they are becoming.

Although Sycamore does have some basic knowledge that they want all graduates to know, in most cases learner outcomes can be mastered while accommodating the learning style and the interests of individual learners.

Sycamore teachers and leaders are all future-focused trend trackers. Their study of the future allows them to update curriculum content when new and relevant content emerges. The same basic skills are then learned utilizing material that has meaning for everyone.

Second languages are valued and expected of all Sycamore graduates.

The Sycamore staff has networking opportunities for curriculum development, reflection on teaching practices, and for continuously improving the learning process.

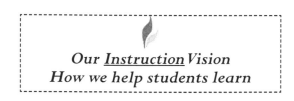

Our _Instruction_ Vision
How we help students learn

Instruction and learning at Sycamore are designed to meet the developmental level, the learning style strength, and the interest area of each student. Students are motivated to learn at their individual maximum pace.

Sycamore offers a safe and secure environment for learning . . . physically, psychologically, and emotionally safe.

Sycamore makes maximum use of technology for learning. As learners advance in our system, more and more of our learner outcomes are mastered by individual students using computers to access challenging and exciting online learning. It is expected that high school students will learn 50% to 60% of their outcomes with technology, leaving teachers time to teach those most important learning outcomes that require a master teacher working with a group of learners.

Because all curriculum is online, anyone can learn most anything, from any place, at any time . . . access to learning is 24/7 for Sycamore learners.

Most learning takes place in real-life/authentic learning contexts where students learn to deal with real-life situations. The community is truly the classroom. Learning and the demonstration of outcome mastery through student projects is a norm at Sycamore.

Learning opportunities often do not follow a single traditional field of study. Most frequently, learners will be learning math, science, language arts, and social science while analyzing and solving real-life problems in today's world.

Because Sycamore customizes learning to the individual student, grade levels have been eliminated. The question is no longer "is Joan ready for the fifth grade" but is "what learning outcome is Joan now ready for."

Sycamore teachers are true professionals who continuously study their craft, reflect on their experiences, and apply the latest and best research regarding learners and learning.

Sycamore teachers connect personally with students, helping to ensure that students find joy in their learning.

Our _Assessment_ Vision
How we measure student success and are held accountable

Student assessment is directly aligned with Sycamore learner outcomes and curriculum. We identify what we want students to know, be able to do, and to be like; we teach to those learner outcomes, and we assess student progress based upon those learning outcomes.

Students are allowed and encouraged to demonstrate their learning in authentic ways. Written tests are not the dominant manner for assessing student learning.

Each Sycamore student creates a multi-media electronic portfolio that documents successful learning. Parents and anyone else with "a need to know" have access to that portfolio in real time.

Meeting individual student learning needs allows Sycamore to have high expectations for student achievement. Our curriculum, instruction, and assessment practices are rigorous, ensuring that our students will be successful in colleges and universities or whatever life they pursue after leaving Sycamore.

Student assessment data is consistently and effectively used to inform students and parents regarding student progress, to provide a feedback loop to teachers regarding teaching strategies, and to help Sycamore teachers and leaders continuously improve student learning results.

Although Sycamore educators do not "teach for the test," Sycamore students perform well when compared to other Illinois schools, when compared nationally, and when compared internationally.

Sycamore graduates/alumni are routinely surveyed, and a significant sample is interviewed in-depth to determine the graduates' perceptions and assessments regarding their educational experiences at Sycamore. Findings from this assessment process are used to continuously improve instruction and learning.

Our *Technology* Vision
How we use technology to customize and increase learning

Every student has access to a computer and the Internet at school and at home.

All Sycamore curriculum can be accessed online 24/7, and students have two or three learning style choices and two or three learning interest choices for most online instruction.

Instruction, available online 24/7, allows individual students and their parents to determine the learner's rate of learning. Anyone can learn anything from anywhere at anytime. Most students advance far beyond the typical curriculum of traditional schools.

Sycamore Information Technology provides easy and effective communication between teachers and parents. Parents, at any time, can access their child's learning records/portfolios, can get tips on how to help their child with his/her present learning challenges, and can view the entire Sycamore set of student learner outcomes.

Sycamore Information Technology makes it possible for each learner throughout the system to have a self-generated Individual Educational Plan (IEP). Learners, with the help of their Learning Coach and parents, schedule their school activities, their learning seminars, their online learner instruction, and their community learning experiences.

This same Information Technology makes it possible for school leaders to track the activities and locations of individual students throughout the day, and provides a system of accountability for school leaders, students, and parents.

Sycamore teachers put as much of their instruction online as possible. When students are learning online, teachers are available to teach those concepts and skills that require group interaction and a professional facilitator.

All technology decisions and purchases . . . hardware and software . . . are based upon the positive impact the technology will have on children.

Our *Stakeholder* Vision
How we involve all members of the community

The mission, vision, and values of the Sycamore Community School District are a direct reflection of the community. The Sycamore community helped to set the Strategic Direction for their school so there is natural support for the vision and core values.

All stakeholders can articulate and enthusiastically support the Sycamore Community School District Mission and Vision.

The Sycamore community serves as a "learning laboratory" for its students and schools. Because the learning outcomes for the Sycamore schools are "life-based," it is natural that the community serves as a learning laboratory for the school. Adults mentor children, businesses open their facilities for student learning, and business/school partnerships allow students to experience the real world.

The Sycamore community provides the resources necessary for the effective operation of its schools. At the same time, the community expects excellent learning opportunities, graduates who are "Empowered Learners Ready to Succeed in Their World," and sound fiscal management.

Sycamore parents are supportive of teachers and the school system. Parents team with the school to ensure that their children receive the best education possible.

Sycamore facilities are first-rate. All learning environments are clean, inviting, and suited for learning.

Our *Personnel* Vision
Who we employ as our ideal staff

The reputation of the Sycamore Community School District for excellence, innovation, and working climate makes it an attractive choice for talented people.

All Sycamore staff, and especially teachers, are hired, empowered, and retained because of their passion for educating children and young adults.

Staff selection, evaluation, and advancement at Sycamore are based on, and directly aligned with, the district's beliefs and values, its mission, and its vision.

Sycamore staff members are true professionals who reflect deeply upon their work — as individuals and as team members — and continually advance their knowledge and professional skills.

Sycamore staff members are caring, kind, consistent, respectful and just in their interactions with students. At the same time, staff members have high expectations and hold high standards for students. This powerful combination of caring and high expectations leads to high levels of student performance.

Teachers and administrators know that students learn in different ways and, sometimes, on different days. They are firm in what learning students must ultimately demonstrate, but they are flexible regarding learning styles and learning rates.

There is a positive and collaborative relationship between the Board of Education, the Leadership Team, teachers, the support staff, and the community. Conflicts do arise, but they are managed in a civil and professional manner with the good of students at the core of all discussions and decisions.

Teachers, administrators, and the support staff take their role as "models for youth" seriously and behave accordingly.

Our <u>Leadership</u> Vision
How we provide support at all levels

Sycamore Community School District leaders are authentic professionals who demonstrate high levels of integrity. They are trustworthy and model ethical and moral behaviors.

Sycamore leaders are future-focused visionaries, with the courage to take risks to improve learning for students.

Sycamore leaders clearly and succinctly articulate and communicate the Sycamore Unified Vision to all groups, and can inform anyone how that vision impacts each staff member within the system. They are effective agents of change who involve everyone in the change process.

Sycamore leaders promote a safe, secure, and trusting learning community that encourages and supports creativity and innovation.

Decisions by the Board of Education and the Leadership Team are always based upon the district's Strategic Design and the short-term and long-term needs of students. Cooperation and support are the norm, and politics do not enter into the decisions of the Board or the Leadership Team.

Sycamore leaders have created an organizational culture that values and rewards student success, staff and student cooperation, innovation, and quality.

Teachers are leaders too, and are recognized as such. Sycamore teachers are involved in the critical decisions that impact their lives and the lives of students.

Leaders at Sycamore consciously and intentionally prepare others for future leadership opportunities.

Sycamore leaders are strong advocates for the district's vision, they speak about it whenever making important decisions, and they signal everyone that the Sycamore Vision is to be consistently and creatively used as a decision screen.

Each of these eight vision components is quite powerful standing alone,
but when considered as a comprehensive and synergistic set,
they point the way to school system transformation...
from School to Learning Community,
from organization focused to learner focused,
from Industrial Age to Age of Empowerment,
and from a one-size-fits-all assembly line to
MASS CUSTOMIZED LEARNING.

From Dreaming to Managing

This is where the heavy lifting must begin. Without consistent and strong leadership from top to bottom, even this inspirational vision will find its way to a dusty shelf. Without forceful expectations for immediate and continuous implementation, expect people, even good people, to quickly fall back into their old routines. It is job #1 for each and every leader throughout the system to help their reports understand the important role they personally play in making this vision a reality. Ken Blanchard reminds us: *"A real vision is lived, not framed."*

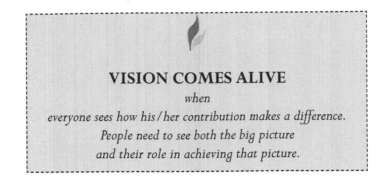

VISION COMES ALIVE
when
everyone sees how his/her contribution makes a difference.
People need to see both the big picture
and their role in achieving that picture.

Implementation is important . . . and anything important should be intentional. Follow-through can't be left to chance. All people, all structures, processes, and policies must be aligned with this vision. Technology purchases and training must be vision based, teacher and principal selection must be vision based, curriculum and instruction must be vision based, and the budget must be vision based. We could go on with this listing, but simply know that anything not aligned with the new vision has to be modified or it has to go. No exceptions. If that sounds tough, well, it has to be. This vision is not about tinkering, it is about transformation. Education is not about waltzing, it's about *"Empowering All Learners to Succeed in Their World,"* which just happens to be Sycamore's mission, its purpose for being.

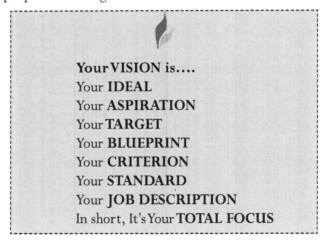

Your VISION is....
Your **IDEAL**
Your **ASPIRATION**
Your **TARGET**
Your **BLUEPRINT**
Your **CRITERION**
Your **STANDARD**
Your **JOB DESCRIPTION**
In short, It's Your **TOTAL FOCUS**

Much more about leadership in Chapter 10, *"Total Leaders."*

Chapter 6
Takeaways:

MCL is not tinkering with today's Industrial Age schools. It is a bold new vision that retains very little of today's practices and structures.

Visions must be concrete to the point that everyone in the system knows how the vision will impact them directly.

The **MCL** vision must be the target, the plan, the goal....in short, the job description and total focus of everyone.

Chapter 7

Lori Does Her Learning Plan/Schedule

*"You can judge your age
by the amount of pain you feel
when you come in contact with a new idea."*

Pearl S. Buck

❧

Chapter 7 Intent

**To clearly demonstrate how
one learner can plan her customized learning schedule . . .
so that everyone can see that the MCL vision can be
operationalized and that the vision is scalable.**

Chapter 7 marks a transition in the nature and intended outcomes of *Inevitable: Mass Customized Learning*. In case you haven't noticed, heretofore we have worked to persuade. We have forcefully and maybe even a bit redundantly told you of the values, philosophy, research, and rationale for implementing **MCL** while sprinkling in a few "how tos." With *"Lori Does Her Learning Plan/Schedule,"* we move our focus to the "how tos," while sprinkling in a bit of seasoned guilt. Guilt that you should/will feel if you don't do what is best for learners and learning which, of course, is **MCL**. In short, do what we tell you, darn it!

Chapter 4, *"Through the Learner's Eyes"* took you through Lori's typical day. Chapter 7 tells how her schedule came to be and begins to identify and describe the transformational technology that enables the personal customization of learning experiences. We again wish to bring your attention to what we believe is the proper role of technology in today's learning communities: technology is not the teacher but the *enabler* of the professional educator. Teachers will always play an important role in the learning process; **MCL** simply makes professionals more efficient with their time and resources.

Make no bones about it. **MCL** will not come easy. Nothing this important seems to come easy. Educators have dreamed about "individualizing instruction" for at least fifty years. If it were easy, we would be doing it now. If it had been possible before, we would be doing it now. But **MCL** will come to be because:

It needs to be done. Our schools must be modernized to take advantage of what today's technology offers. We must begin to meet the learning needs of tomorrow and not continue to focus on the needs of the past. And we simply have to become more effective and efficient in doing what we do.

It can be done. What we are proposing couldn't have been done ten years ago. The "customizing technology" didn't exist until now. But it is here now and it has been proven. All that needs to be done is to transfer the technology now in place in other innovative organizations/businesses to school systems.

**It will be done.** When the NetGeners are in control of school systems . . . all types of systems for that matter . . . they will quickly integrate what they know about learners, learning, and learning organizations with the transformational technologies that they have experienced their entire life. **MCL** makes too much sense to not become a reality. You might even say that it's _Inevitable_.

LORI'S 60-DAY LEARNING PLAN

My Dad introduced me to you in Chapter 4, "Through the Learner's Eyes," but to help you remember how he described me, let me again share his rather idealistic description.....there are things that even Dad doesn't know:

> _* 14 years old, parents are both educators, middle class_
> _* Quite responsible....but a teenager_
> _* Interested in pop music, athletics, math, and technology_
> _* Knows that she is college bound_
> _* Thinks Christopher is "cool"_

I am working through my learning program at the Lincoln Unlimited Learning Center. The LULC serves about 4,000 learners from four- and five-year-old preschoolers to 17- and 18-year-olds who are completing their programs. Our schools have changed significantly over the past few years. Five years ago the community went through a future-focused planning process that resulted in a school name change and a new way of scheduling our learning activities. Today we all have individual learning plans, and based on our past behavior and accomplishments, my friends and I have a lot to say about our learning schedule.

I am doing my schedule for the first two months, and I will explain what I am doing and why I am doing it. There are a few learners in our learning community who have their schedules planned for them, but most everyone has gradually learned to do their own planning as they progress through their learner outcomes. We are the only school system in our area that is doing MASS CUSTOMIZED LEARNING _but we are getting many visitors who want to learn about how our learning community operates._

**MCL** works well for my friends and me. We go through the learner outcomes at our own pace and most of the graduates of LULC are well ahead of those who graduated from the old program that moved everyone along at the same pace.

> *Today is August 1 and I will be planning my schedule for September and October. I have found it best to schedule my learning activities in advance so that I can get into the seminars I want and my friends and I can coordinate our activities. I like to stay at least one month ahead with my schedule.*
>
> *I talk with my Mom and Dad about my schedule all the time and they make suggestions as to what I should do . . . actually, they probably have veto power but it never seems to come to that. Ms. Trezona is my learning coach and she definitely has veto power over my schedule. Ms. Trezona knows me well. She has coached me for the past two years and I actually got to pick her to be my coach. She is a tough cookie with high expectations and I actually like her for that!*
>
> *Today I am doing my schedule with my Dad. I pretty well know what I will do but Dad wants to be involved and sometimes he has pretty good ideas. Ms. Trezona does not think that she has to be involved in planning my schedule, but she will review it and respond soon after I hit "send."*
>
> *Step 1 is for me to review my learning portfolio. What learner outcomes have I completed and which outcomes should I be attending to next? All LULC learner outcomes matched to my electronic learning portfolio are available online from the LULC web page.*

System Structures/Practices Supporting Lori's Plan

What made Lori's scheduling process possible? What did the LULC do to create the systems that allow Lori to create her schedule for the next 60 days?

1. The leaders of LULC completed the Strategic Design process described in Chapter 3 that identified the exit learner outcomes for their graduates. Not a simple task, but one that is meaningful and doable.
2. The Curriculum and Instruction people of the organization . . . with input from teachers of course . . . worked back from the exit learner outcomes to create enabling outcomes for all levels of learning. Not a simple task, but one that is necessary and doable.
3. The Information Technology people . . . with input from the curriculum and instruction people and teachers of course . . . created an electronic

portfolio system that automatically documents the learner performances that are required for proof of learner mastery. Not an easy task but one that has been accomplished by some learning systems.

With some coaching from Ms. Trezona, I have learned that there is a planning sequence that saves me from having to make major revisions just when I think that I am about finished with my schedule. The tip: first schedule those activities that are the least flexible and cannot be easily changed, and save the flexible stuff for the end. I love gymnastics, I do all-around, and I compete for the LULC gymnastics team. Gymnastics is my most rigidly scheduled activity so I will schedule it first. Practice is from 3:30 to 5:00 Monday through Friday except for the days when we have meets scheduled. It's a simple process to schedule my practices and my meets when most of my days are blank.

What did the LULC do to create the systems that allow Lori to create this part of her schedule?

1. LULC creates and publishes an annual online calendar of events that includes everything learners will have to know to create their personal schedules. The calendar includes all scheduled gymnastics meets.

2. The system has adopted the Microsoft Exchange Calendar throughout the system. (They could have chosen a scheduling calendar from a number of competing companies, but designating one specific calendar makes the integration of calendars more friction free.)

3. Lori's schedule is made available to anyone "with a need to know" . . . and those with a need to know will have a password that ensures privacy. Lori, her parents, her learning coach, and the LULC principal are designated as people "with a need to know."

The next least flexible type of learning activity at LULC is the in-depth seminars that are designed around complex learner outcomes that require interaction between the learning facilitator and me and between my classmates and me. You might recall from Chapter 3 that I want to schedule:

- the Interpersonal Communications seminar (a 30-hour commitment)
- the Diversity seminar (a 24-hour commitment) and

- *the Creating and Defending a Business Plan seminar (a 27-hour commitment)*

After thinking it over, I think that I could also complete
- *the Forms of Government seminar (a 20-hour commitment)*

during the next 60 days . . . it will crowd my calendar a bit but three of my friends . . . including Christopher are scheduling it too.

Each of the four seminars I want to take is scheduled at least once during September and October. I will schedule those that are only offered once first and hope that I get them . . . you can see now why I like to do my scheduling at least a month before the activity is to happen. If I can't get the seminars I want when I want them because they are filled, I will schedule them next time they are offered so I can be sure to complete them sometime soon. Well here goes, wish me luck . . . and wish my friends luck too because we are trying to get into the same seminars.

What did the LULC do to create the systems that allow Lori to create this part of her schedule?

1. The curriculum and instruction people . . . input from teachers of course . . . went through all of the LULC learner outcomes and answered the following question for each of them, "How is this learner outcome best learned?" A **most important question!**

2. For those learner outcomes best learned online with a computer, they identified or created online learning opportunities. These online learning activities, including a built-in learner assessment, were made available on the LULC web page 24/7. More, and more sophisticated, online learning programs are being developed every day. Most systems will not have to reinvent the wheel. (It is important that as many learner outcomes as possible be placed in the "online learning" category. The middle and high schools with whom we have worked estimate that a minimum of 50% to 60% of what we now teach could be learned effectively online. The more learners can learn online, the more time ~~teachers~~ learning facilitators will have to teach the outcomes that require the professional working with small groups of learners.)

3. For those learner outcomes best learned in a seminar format, the curriculum and instruction people . . . with much input from specific teachers of course . . . developed seminars much like colleges and universities create, describe, and schedule courses. Each seminar topic can be directly traced to an exit learner outcome and to one or more Spheres of Living from the Strategic Design planning process.

4. The online seminar-scheduling program is coordinated with the individual learner's scheduling process. If the Interpersonal Communications seminar only accommodates 18 learners and it has been filled, anyone attempting to schedule that seminar will be informed that the seminar is filled and informed of other available dates with openings.

> *Much of my science is online . . . even many of my experiments are conducted via virtual reality. But there are things that our science learning facilitators want done in the science lab and I enjoy that. It gives me a chance to meet other learners and to actually touch things. Scheduling my science lab time is usually quite easy. Scheduling lab time seems to be more flexible than scheduling seminars. So after I have my seminars scheduled I block out times to be in the science lab.*
>
> *Some of the lab work requires preparation so when I get to a certain place in my online learning outcomes, I am automatically informed of when that lab experience will be offered. I look for empty spaces in my schedule and schedule lab times at times and places that are easy to coordinate with my other activities of the day. After doing my schedule for a couple of years I have learned how to save time and travel.*

What did the LULC do to create the systems that allow Lori to create this part of her schedule?

1. Virtual reality has made it possible to conduct many experiments online. But for those learning activities requiring labs and other hands-on experiences, the curriculum and instruction people . . . with input from specific teachers of course . . . create, describe, and schedule activities much like science labs in high schools and universities and much like our best Technical Training Institutes. These hands-on learning experiences can be scheduled much like the seminars described above except that the location of the learning activity, by its nature, must be more site specific.

2. Seminar and lab attendance is monitored. Attendance is taken at all sessions and parents are automatically contacted and informed about a learner absence. Learning Community leaders know where each student is to be at any time of the day. Their name or number is entered into the master schedule program, which instantly brings up their daily schedule including activities and locations.

> *Doing online learning by yourself makes it easy to schedule . . . I am the only one I need to be concerned about, but it can be a bit boring after awhile. I have three good friends . . . all girls with whom I do my online math. We all are at about the same place in math and we go at about the same speed. We have fun of course and we help each other when one of us needs some quick tutoring. We set aside 6 to 8 hours each week to work together on math . . . we find a time that fits into all of our schedules by using our Microsoft scheduling calendars to automatically find times when all four of us are free. Sometimes we do our work in the learning community computer lab and sometimes we meet in one of our homes. We live close to each other and often coordinate our travel time. Everyone at LULC has a laptop and access to the Internet of course.*

What did the LULC do to create the systems that allow Lori to create this part of her schedule?

1. The Microsoft Exchange Calendar makes it possible to coordinate the personal calendars. This technology is also available from many other IT companies. The LULC would have to make that service available to all staff and all learners.

> *The LULC is very good about meeting my learning needs, but there are some things that I want to learn and want to do that don't fit into the **MCL** program. When I have something that I want to do and don't know how to go about it I schedule a time to discuss it with Ms. Trezona. For instance, because I have an interest in music and want to learn how businesses work, I would like to do a project that would help me to learn about how the music business works. I doubt that I will ever be an entertainer, but I think that I might be interested in a career in the business side of the music industry.*

My Mom has a friend who works at a bank who used to be a professional entertainer in the pop music field. I have talked with Mom's friend and she seemed excited to think that she might mentor me in my study of the music industry . . . her banking experience would help with the financial part of the industry and she too was looking forward to learning more about what I wanted to learn about.

One of our learner outcomes from the Economic Sphere of Living is about business plans. Although the LULC has a seminar on that outcome I am allowed to do a personal project in place of that seminar as long as I can demonstrate the learner outcomes. Ms. Trezona has the authority to OK that project for me and she has agreed to facilitate a planning meeting between my mentor and me. I am really excited about it; who knows, one day I might be a talent scout! I have a friend who is thinking about joining me in this project. Christopher is interested in this topic too.

What did the LULC do to create the systems that allow Lori to create this part of her schedule?

1. The key to this type of flexibility lies in writing learner outcomes that are demonstrations of learning. That is, outcomes that are clear about what the learner must do to demonstrate mastery of that learning outcome. Traditional curriculum tends to be about "topics, about what the course will cover."

2. This type of flexibility will be difficult to find in school systems that do not have a learner centered, outcome based, open and flexible culture. Creating that culture is everyone's responsibility but it must involve and begin with the system's leaders.

3. We frequently hear phrases like "the community is our school" which usually means that people volunteer to help out in classrooms. A good thing; but that's not what we are suggesting here. A real Learning Community goes far beyond that and it does it intentionally and systematically. Economic seminars take place at the bank and bank directors facilitate; biology seminars take place in hospitals and are facilitated by doctors and nurses; and mentors from all professions and occupations are eager to coach a young learner through a meaningful and real project.

> *The last thing I put on my learning calendar is the online outcomes that I do by myself and can schedule at my convenience. Mom and Dad think that it is best if I schedule my days much like someone with a regular job would do, which means a minimum of a 40-hour week. I carry my Netbook wherever I go and so I can work on my online learner outcomes whenever I have the time . . . but I do schedule them in advance to stop me from getting lazy.*
>
> *I can also work on the online outcomes from anywhere, which helps a lot with my schedule. My preference is to work on them at home but I find that many times I have gaps in my schedule when it would be difficult and time consuming to get home and then back to another activity. So most of the time I just try to find a quiet place, open my Netbook, call up my learner portfolio and go for it. Our Learning Community has many places where we can work online. Even businesses seem to like to see us working in their places. Internet hotspots are everywhere . . . wish I could afford Starbucks more often.*
>
> *My friends and I have become a little competitive about our progress. I think that my three girlfriends and I will complete all of the exit learner outcomes and be eligible for graduation before we are seventeen. That is our target anyway.*

What did the LULC do to create the systems that allow Lori to create this part of her schedule?

1. Earlier in this chapter we described what the Learning Community must do to make their online learning activities available for learners 24/7. Selecting or creating, organizing, testing, and making online learning activities available is a large task and must be one of the first projects initiated soon after a **MCL** vision has been agreed upon. The good news is that there are already good programs available and more are being created all the time. Learning Communities, educators, and learners will soon have alternatives for most learner outcomes that are common to curriculum. Today's digital world has made choice ubiquitous.

2. Credit card companies have programs to determine the amount customers must pay on their account each month and customers are contacted . . . and probably threatened if the minimum amount is not paid. Walmart has a computerized system to know exactly when one of their

products must be ordered to ensure that the product will continue to be available to customers. That type of technology could easily be used to determine when individual learners are falling behind on their online learner outcomes. Learning systems will want to implement a feedback loop that will automatically inform "those with a need to know," including parents of course, when a learner is not meeting expectations. They will also want to inform the "need to knowers" when a learner is exceeding expectations. And the acceptable rates of progress can differ for learners. Not all learners learn at the same rate. The danger will be in having lower expectations for some learners simply because of their socio-economic status or some other indefensible criterion.

So there it is, my learning schedule for September and October. You can see everything that I hope to accomplish these two months. My Dad has given it an OK and I will now hit "send" and it will go to Ms. Trezona, my learning coach, my Mom and Dad's inbox, my gymnastics coach, all of the seminar and lab learning facilitators whose learning activities I have scheduled, and to the Learning Community Central Office. The only one on my list that may want me to make a change in my schedule will be Ms. Trezona, and she always gets back to me right away if she thinks I should make a change.

My parents, who refer to themselves as "digital immigrants," are afraid that I might depend on the computer and the Internet too much, and that I won't have enough opportunities to interact and work with other kids. So Dad and I always do a check of my learning plan to see if we can keep it about 50 – 50. It doesn't have to be exact but he wants me to have about the same amount of time with group experiences as with individual online learning.

Letting the Fast Runners Run

You may think that Lori is an exceptional kid and that there aren't many like her, but in our experiences as teachers and principals, there are a lot of Loris out there who only need to have the ceiling on learning removed so they can excel far beyond what they now are allowed and encouraged to do. We confidently estimate that if **MCL** were a reality for our learners, far more than 50% of our students would outdistance what the top 5% now accomplish. When we combine the learner motivation that is fostered by **MCL** with the tools to learn that encourage rather than impede acceleration, test scores are sure to rise significantly. And a love for learning is retained.

And none of this is at the expense of the slower learner. They too will have their daily learning needs met without the stigma of being in a special program. They too would most likely see their motivation and achievement increase. Although we believe that today's schools place too much emphasis on high stakes testing, we believe that composite test scores in the United States would increase to the point that we would again lead the world in learner achievement. The potential of **MCL** is great.

Restating the Purpose of <u>*Inevitable*</u>

There is much to agree upon in regard to education and much on which to disagree. Not everyone agrees on the *purpose* of education. At one end of the continuum we have those who would like a rigorous traditional curriculum, a curriculum determined by the state or by a blue ribbon committee. Would **MCL** work for these people? On the other end of that continuum, there are those who prefer learning opportunities that focus on the "whole child," learning opportunities that cater to the unique talents, gifts, and interests of the individual learner. Would **MCL** work for these people?

As regards degree of *control*, there are those who believe that schools need to be very directive, that adults should determine what is learned, when it is learned, how it is learned and how students should be assessed. Would **MCL** work for these people? At the other end of the control continuum, there are those who believe strongly that learners should be allowed choices of the what, when, and how of learning . . . and at a relatively young age. Would **MCL** work for these people? There are strong beliefs and feelings along both the *purpose of education* and *degree of control* continuums.

Our intent is not to convince you as to the purpose of education, nor is it to suggest the level of control adults should have over the learning process.

> **Our intent** *is that you become convinced that the Industrial Age, assembly line delivery of instruction is wrong for learners and educators alike and that there is a better . . . a MUCH BETTER . . . way!*

Once you break free of the assembly line and all of the negative controls that this outdated format puts on your options, you will be free to customize in any fashion you choose. You can design a learning system that fits on either the purpose or the control continuum. We of course have our own personal biases as to the purpose and control issues, but those are not what we are preaching or promoting. We are not telling you what to do, we are telling you what to stop doing. Stop doing assembly line learning! We are not imposing anything other than a much more efficient and effective learning model that is flexible enough to meet your community's beliefs and aspirations.

Chapter 7
Takeaways:

The technology to create personalized schedules/agendas exists and is easy to manipulate. Hard to create and organize for sure . . . but easy for the user to manipulate.

Once the organizational infrastructure for **MCL** is in place, the technical part of creating a personalized learning schedule is relatively easy . . . it's the importance and critical nature of the decisions that require time and deep thought.

MCL moves control and responsibility from the educator to the learner . . . and in the process creates Self-Directed, LifeLong Learners.

Chapter 8

Weight Bearing Walls

*"Your organization is perfectly structured
to get the results that you are now getting."*

"Leaving the past is central to progress."

Peter Drucker

Chapter 8 Intent

**To convince educational leaders
that they can remain in control of a MCL system . . .
that they can be accountable for
the learning, supervision, and safety needs of learners
while providing customized learning experiences for all.**

Note Significant parts of this chapter have been adapted from Spady and Schwahn's book titled Learning Communities 2.0, written for the American Association of School Administrators and available from Rowman and Littlefield Publishing Company.

Any organization made up of two or more people requires a "structure" for getting things done, and the larger the organization, the more complex the structure . . . usually. When organizations are running smoothly and getting things done without friction, people seldom talk about their organizational structure. They may not even be consciously aware of the structure. Their response to "Can you describe the structure of your organization?" might be "huh?" But when the organizational structure is getting in the way of efficiency and effectiveness, the astute thinker will analyze the problem to determine if the organizational structure is compatible with, and facilitating of, the goals of the system.

Worst case scenario . . . the organizational structure is not facilitating of organization goals but no one notices because the organizational structure is taken as a given. "We have always done it this way" . . . *assumption,* and we always will. Unfortunately, today's school systems fall into the "worst case scenario" of our organizational structure discussion.

We, and this is a collective we . . . . educators, parents, business people, even STUDENTS and TECHNOLOGY GURUS . . . cannot think "outside the box" when it comes to analyzing the Industrial Age, assembly line structure of our schools. We have this vision of one of Steve Jobs's children attending a school in which all fourth graders are listening to the same teacher, irrespective of individual learner needs, and not questioning the structure of schools. But when he thinks music, he thinks specific songs for specific people, available from iTunes 24/7, heard on any one of fifteen listening devices which Apple provides, and listening to that song from anywhere at any time. *Excuse me Steve, but could I have a little more bass on that Susan Boyle one?*

Succinctly put:

☑ *Today's bureaucratic public schools are structured for administrative convenience;*

☑ *Our instructional delivery system does not consider learner motivation;*

☑ *The system makes it very difficult for teachers to act as professionals; and*

☑ *We all act as though we don't know it!*

About Weight Bearing Walls (WBW)

In case you have not caught it, the title of this chapter, "*Weight Bearing Walls*," is a metaphor we will use to help us understand the need for organizational structure, and how organizational structures can be directly aligned with the goals of the organization. In this case, to create a structure that promotes meeting the individual learning needs of every learner every hour of every day. In short, how to create a structure that facilitates MASS CUSTOMIZED LEARNING.

So follow the logic of the following list regarding optimizing organizational structure, and then we will get on with using the WBW metaphor to show how we can move school systems from the bureaucratic, Industrial Age WBWs to the mass customized, Information Age WBWs.

Organizations Require Structures:

Things need to be accomplished. Things need to get done.

People need to know where they are to be, what they are to do . . . and all of that, of course, has to fit with what everyone else is doing.

There is a need to coordinate work/activity with space and resources.

There needs to be a system of accountability . . . both internal and external accountability.

Organizational structure is most effective and efficient when there is no friction between the structure and the optimum use of resources.

Lest this discussion of organizational structure seems too complicated or too lofty, we would like to point out that soccer moms, with all their responsibilities and activities, are very skilled at accomplishing the five points listed above. We think that they just might use a different vocabulary . . . like, "Let's just use a little common sense here. There is a better way of doing this. What if we . . ."

Our picture of an "ideal best" instructional delivery system (**MCL**) had its beginning several years ago when we were asked to work with Doug Parks and about seventy of his superintendent colleagues from Lake County, Illinois. The term *"mass customization"* was finding its way into the futures, change, and leadership literature at that time, and we were asked to explore with them whether the technology that made it possible for businesses to deliver customized products and services might be transferable to education. *In other words, might schools be able to mass customize learning?* After our presentation and considerable discussion in small groups, the group readily acknowledged that our present assembly line learning system was outdated, ineffective, and in need of significant change; and, they weren't defensive or offended when we compared education practices to business practices.

We designed the seminar around the metaphor of "Weight Bearing Walls" (WBWs). Think of them as the walls that keep our Industrial Age system in place and make it nearly impossible to change. Our challenge was to show them how transformational technologies could replace all of those seemingly "essential walls" with new structural supports that would facilitate **MCL** and paradigm change. So we offered the following observations:

- The roofs of buildings are held up by walls. Some are "weight bearing," others are not. Construction managers must know the difference because . . .
- If you remove a WBW, the roof will collapse, destroying the structure and probably causing severe injury to everyone involved.
- To safely remove a WBW, one must first replace it with another device that safely supports the roof.

Schools, like other organizations, also have operational WBWs that support their present purpose and patterns of functioning, and that can safely be replaced with other supporting devices.

Once we understood and embraced the analytic power of the WBW metaphor, we asked the starter questions:

"What are the WBWs that are not allowing us to change, to update and restructure education, to bring our industry/profession into the Information Age?

What are the WBWs that are holding up our outdated and leaking roof?

What are the walls (present structures, processes, and practices) that, even if one were removed, might cause it all to come crashing down?"

In other words......

"What are the greatest change fears of principals and superintendents?"

The fun started. Seventy superintendents in small groups knew they were onto something important. They seemed to drop all defensiveness. No "ya buts" were heard . . . or allowed. Each group of 7 or 8 started their list of WBWs. Lists were combined, clarified, and agreed upon. After about two hours of energized work, the Lake County superintendents had identified the WBWs that were the most significant and also the most resistant to change.

They then reached consensus on the ten major/significant WBWs that "hold up" our present school and school system "roofs." (As you might expect, we have tweaked the WBW labels and the structures they provide just a bit to make our points.)

Be aware of our intent here: *to shift your thinking.* Once you finish reflecting on these ten Industrial Age WBWs, we want you to be thinking and saying things like the following:

1) *These are the WBWs that hold up our organizational structure . . . and I see why we need them;*
2) *Although we need these Industrial Age WBWs, they also stop us from doing some things that WE KNOW ARE RIGHT FOR LEARNERS;*
3) *OK, HALLELUJAH, now that we have mass customizing transformational technologies that can hold up our school system roof, we can do what we know is best for learners without the roof falling in on us . . . and we can be more professional while doing it;*
4) *So what's stopping us? I'll sign on to* MASS CUSTOMIZED LEARNING *and will lobby my friends and colleagues. Now that I know that* **MCL** *doesn't mean "technology as teacher," but technology as "enabler," it all makes sense to me.*

1. GRADE LEVELS

What they do for us:................... Allow us to group students and to move them through the twelve-year cycle

What they stop us from doing:...... Allowing all learners to progress at their optimum rate of learning

Today's enabling technology:........ Allows for the mass customization of products and services

Who is doing it now:................. Apple iTunes, Google, Amazon.com, Bing

2. STUDENTS ASSIGNED TO CLASSROOMS

What they do for us:................... Allow us to divide/group students into manageable numbers and to assign staff responsible for control and accountability

What they stop us from doing:...... Bringing students with similar learning needs together with a master teacher to study and master a specific learner outcome

Today's power technology:........... Allows for complex schedule coordination

Who is doing it now:................. Microsoft Exchange Calendar, Yahoo! Calendar, Google Calendar, Apple iCal

3. CLASS PERIODS/BELL SCHEDULE

What they do for us:................. Provide logistical control of curriculum, courses, staff and students....we always know where everyone is....or should be

What they stop us from doing:......	Putting everyone....learners and teachers....in control of getting to where they need to be
Today's power technology:...........	Allows for complex schedule coordination
Who is doing it now:..................	Microsoft Exchange Calendar, Yahoo! Calendar, Google Calendar, Apple iCal

4. COURSES/CURRICULUM

What they do for us:...................	Identify what we will teach/cover, and divides the content into chunks that fit into quarters, semesters, years, and ultimately into graduation requirements
What they stop us from doing:......	Allowing life-role learner outcomes to determine the direction and progress of learning
Today's power technology:...........	Allows any content to be available from anywhere at any time
Who is doing it now:..................	Wikipedia, Bing, Google, the Web

5. TEXTBOOKS

What they do for us:...................	Provide authoritative and dependable content/curriculum in chunks that fit a specific course...teachers know what to teach and students know what they are to learn
What they stop us from doing:......	Accessing nearly unlimited content from anywhere that directly fits learner needs and interests
Today's power technology:...........	Virtually all known information is readily available on the Internet
Who is doing it now:..................	Bing, Google, Yahoo, Wikipedia

6. PAPER AND PENCIL

What they do for us:.................... Provide written documentation/records of the performance and achievement of students

What they stop us from doing:...... Using digital records of student performance that are easily reconfigured into different formats

Today's power technology:........... Thumb drives which hold 8 gigs of data

Who is doing it now:................. Thumb drives and larger digital storage devices available in all electronic stores, Target, Walmart.....computer backup drives store and protect great amounts of information

7. ABC GRADING SYSTEM

What it does for us:................... Allows us to evaluate the progress of all students, rank/compare their achievement, and determine those who have met graduation requirements

What it stops us from doing:...... Allowing each student to create an electronic portfolio documenting his/her outcome demonstrations

Today's power technology:........... Personal production of all types of media....with rather good quality....by anyone with a computer and digital camera

Who is doing it now:................. YouTube, MySpace, Facebook..... and many, many people from their homes or offices

8. REPORT CARDS

What they do for us:...................	Allow us to evaluate the performance/achievement of students and communicate that evaluation to parents
What they stop us from doing:......	Providing learners, parents, and teachers real- time information regarding real student achievement
Today's power technology:...........	Secure, encrypted digital communication with anyone "with a need to know"
Who is doing it now:...................	Banks, online retailers, Amazon. com, eBay

9. LEARNING HAPPENS IN SCHOOLS

What it does for us:...................	Allows the school system to be in control of students, to create a system of accountability for the physical well-being of learners, and to efficiently administer a logistically complex organization
What it stops us from doing:......	Learning in real-life contexts, making effective use of community resources....both physical and human resources
Today's power technology:...........	Allows anyone to learn anything from anywhere at any time from worldwide resources
Who is doing it now:...................	Phoenix University and other online learning courses and degrees, cyber schools, exchange programs, mentoring programs, learner "shadowing" opportunities

10. NINE-MONTH SCHOOL YEAR

What it does for us:	Allows parents to schedule vacations and have the youngsters home to help harvest crops (having a little fun here, but no one could come up with any reason other than "tradition")
What it stops us from doing:	Continuous learning and development. . . . eliminating learning regression
Today's power technology:	Nearly all types of business, and especially "knowledge work" is conducted from anywhere in the world 24/7/365
Who is doing it now:	Virtually all online information sources and businesses; in short, anyone in the US born after 1980. . . .and the majority of Sun City, AZ retirees

OK now, everyone, all together . . . "I 'get it.' All organizations require WBWs, but we can replace our Industrial Age WBWs with Information Age WBWs; our roof won't collapse and we can at long last accomplish our professional goal of personalizing learning to each learner."

The Proof is in the Pudding

If **MCL** is to happen, it will happen because secondary principals want it to happen and, probably even more importantly, believe that they can make it happen without losing control of the school. It's not that they lack courage or are afraid to take a risk, but because secondary principals must be practical and pragmatic about control. Show us a secondary principal not able to control his/her school and we'll show you a principal, head down, and heading out the door.

This WBW chapter and the following two chapters are about getting concrete about a new organizational structure for schools, about a new structure that will foster personalized learning programs for each learner. This section of

Inevitable is intended to convince the secondary principal that she/he can imple-ment **MCL**, remain in control, hold her/his job . . . and maybe even become a hero/heroine for professionalizing education. We know that **MCL** is desirable, doable and destined to happen . . . it is after all, _INEVITABLE._

Chapter 8
Takeaways:

Industrial Age WBWs must be replaced by Information Age WBWs . . . the control necessary for security and accountability remains.

Form still follows function . . . only after we have determined what we want our graduates to demonstrate can we determine the organizational structure that best makes that happen.

Powerful technology to replace the Industrial Age structure of schools and school systems with Information Age structures exists today, and that technology is proving itself effective in our everyday lives.

"You never change things by fighting the existing reality.
To change something, build a new model that
makes the existing model obsolete."

Buckminster Fuller

Chapter 9

Ready for Rollout

It's almost unbelievable today, but . . . .

It took centuries for someone to connect
suitcase technology with wheel technology.

Can you still buy a suitcase without wheels?

Today, the Industrial Age school system is the suitcase,
and mass customizing technology is the wheels.

Chapter 9 Intent

To clearly identify the systems and processes
that must be in place prior to the successful implementation
of the MASS CUSTOMIZED LEARNING vision . . .
to provide a checklist of those systems,
processes, and technologies
required for the successful launch of
MASS CUSTOMIZED LEARNING.

MASS CUSTOMIZED LEARNING is a new concept, a new paradigm if you wish. Probably viewed by some as radical. To understand and ultimately embrace the **MCL** vision, we think it is helpful to look at it from a number of perspectives. When you do, we trust that you will not think it radical at all. New, innovative, and different maybe, but not radical.

Chapter 4 showed how **MCL** looks to the learner one day at a time. Chapter 6 provided a detailed verbal description of the **MCL** vision. Chapter 7 provided a learning plan perspective as Lori created her schedule. Chapter 8 should have given us confidence when we were able to learn how the Industrial Age weight bearing walls could effectively be replaced by transformational technology without the roof falling in. Chapter 9 takes us a level below these four perspectives to identify the infrastructure requirements that hold up **MCL**, that make it doable, that make it ready to roll out, that someday will make it look smooth, seamless, and . . . "a piece of cake." (Note: McGarvey and Schwahn tend to be optimists. The glass IS actually *more than* half full.)

Infrastructure? . . . examples

"Infrastructure" is not a frequently used term. Not in our company anyway, so we would like to help you understand what we mean when we write infrastructure. A few concrete examples may define the term best:

We have probably all ridden in elevators numerous times. When I (cjs) first met an elevator . . . and had not yet learned elevator etiquette, but that's another story . . . I wondered how it worked. I knew the "what" of elevators, knew what it did for me, but the "how" of elevators was a mystery, an intriguing mystery. Maybe this is just a boy thing, but I immediately wondered, and wanted to know, how it worked. You too? Have you ever wondered about how elevators work . . wondered about the "infrastructure" of elevators, the gears, the cables, the weights? Much like you might be wondering about the "infrastructure" that will make **MCL** *work as smoothly as the elevator? Then one day I walked into a very modern library, and there in the middle of a spacious first floor was an elevator, an elevator totally enclosed in glass. You could see the gears, the cables, the weights and all. Imagine my excitement . . . am I overdoing this thing a bit . . . when I stepped into the glass cubical and pushed "2"? I saw how it all worked. I saw the "inner workings" of the elevator. Although complex, the system was logical and understandable . . . and much of the mystery of the elevator disappeared. I had a similar experience the first time I saw a moving sidewalk under repair. The repair persons (note the PC label) had exposed and were working on the sidewalk's infrastructure; I could see the stuff that made the sidewalk move.*

FedEx and UPS are another good example of a complex infrastructure that seems to work smoothly . . . most of the time.

Imagine if you could see behind the scenes of what it really takes for me to choose a book on Amazon.com on Sunday evening, click on the "buy with one click" button, pay for the book via Visa, be told daily on my computer where my book actually is in real time, and have the book delivered by UPS at my front door in Phoenix on Tuesday.

A bit more complex than a soccer mom planning her day, but not that different at their "logistical planning" core.

Seven Critical Elements....Ready for Rollout

Much of what is contained in this chapter has been alluded to in the preceding chapters as we described **MCL** and attempted to provide evidence that the technology necessary to make it work already exists and has been proven to be efficient and effective in other businesses and industries. But what follows is a detailed checklist of the seven critical elements that must be in place before the leaders of a school system can confidently begin **MCL** for all learners. "Ready for rollout" in today's rapidly changing world means that all is in place. That systems have been tested, everyone knows their roles, and we are ready to please customers when we open the door. Ready for rollout means that your school system: . . . .

1. Has derived a strategic design (SD)
2. Has written curriculum as Learner Outcomes
3. Has categorized Learner Outcomes by learning format
4. Has created and placed online Learner Outcomes online
5. Has created seminars for those Learner Outcomes requiring an interactive seminar format
6. Has designed and implemented scheduling technology for individual learners
7. Has designed and implemented accountability technology for administration

1. The School System Has Derived a Strategic Design (SD)

This first component of the **MCL** vision is not technology driven. It is *consensus building* driven, *support building* driven. Chapter 3, *"But First . . . Our Purpose"* outlines the process for what we have labeled Strategic Design, a process that involves meaningful participation of all significant role groups in determining the direction and purpose of the school system. (More on the leader's role in deriving a Strategic Design in the next chapter, *"Total Leaders."*) In short, the SD process provides direction by identifying the organization's core values, its mission/purpose, exit learner outcomes, and a detailed vision of what the system will be like when operating at its ideal best. Chapter 6, *"**MCL**: The Vision (Detailed)"* provides a concrete example of a comprehensive vision created by a school district. Setting the Strategic Direction is the obvious starting point for creating meaningful and productive change.

Note that we label this component "_Derived_ a Strategic Plan." "_Creating_ a Strategic Plan" would not have been quite right. The SD planning process begins with a study of the future, and the entire process is future focused, systematic, and logical. The Strategic Direction does not come out of thin air, but is _derived_ through an in-depth study of the future and a thorough analysis of what it will take for learners to succeed in the rapidly changing world they will encounter after graduation.

2. The School System Has Written Curriculum as Learner Outcomes

We have already written some about the advantages of writing curriculum as outcomes rather than as content to be covered/studied, but let's talk more about learner outcomes in the context of the **MCL** infrastructure. Learner outcomes are critical to individual and organizational accountability. If we are not clear about what we want graduates to know, do, and be like, how can it be measured and, therefore, how can our school systems be accountable?

Now we are well aware that some of the most powerful learning outcomes are difficult to measure, but learner outcomes as we write them are demonstrations of learning. Not all . . . actually, not many . . . are pencil and paper tests. Outcomes as subjective and complex as "creating and sustaining healthy relationships" or "writing and defending a business plan" can . . . actually must . . . be demonstrated to be valid.

The Strategic Design process (#1 above) identified the exit learner outcomes for each Sphere of Living (see Chapter 3). Each Sphere of Living includes from 6 to 12 rather general learner outcomes. The logic here is that when graduates are able to demonstrate each of the exit outcomes for each of the seven or eight Spheres of Living, they would leave our system "empowered to be successful in a rapidly changing world." Which ~~may be~~ should be the mission/purpose of our school system.

But those exit outcomes are broad and general, too broad and general to be learned easily or in short time periods. Therefore, each of the exit outcomes needs to be supported by "enabling outcomes" that then serve as the school system's curriculum. Got IT!! Four-year olds, ten-year olds, sixteen-year olds are all learning to demonstrate "enabling outcomes" that are aligned with and supportive of the exit learner outcomes. Although this structure may appear to be rigid and controlling, it is not. **MCL**, as you know from previous chapters, puts the learner at the center of learning. The learner's learning activities are tailored to his/her current level of learning, to his/her learning style, and to his/her arenas of interest.

3. The School System Has Categorized Learner Outcomes by Learning Format

Learner outcomes, as you learned earlier, are demonstrations of learning. We know quite clearly, and in advance, what the learner is to do to show evidence that he/she has mastered the intended learner outcome. And to be truly learner centered, which **MCL** is of course, the question that follows "What's the intended learner outcome?" is "How is that learner outcome best learned?" This question and this infrastructure component focus learning on the learner, and it also sets the school system up to be able to create the process for personalizing each learner's learning schedule. This will become clear when we get to critical element 6, Designing and Implementing Scheduling Technology for Learners.

About Learning Format Options

To be able to answer the "*how is this outcome best learned*" question, we must first identify the learning options that we will have at our ready. To explain the process, we have chosen the following learning alternatives:

> ONLINE LEARNING: *those learner outcomes learned most efficiently and effectively via electronics . . . a computer and the Internet.*

> SEMINARS: *where we bring learners together with a learning facilitator to learn those outcomes that require interaction, give-and-take, questioning, modeling, practicing, etc.*

> LAB WORK: *those outcomes that require hands-on experiments or experiences . . . typically associated with science, technical training, and building trades.*

> PROJECTS: *for those learner outcomes that are best learned by actually doing something, creating something, solving a problem. Project might be designed by and for individuals, or for small- to medium-sized groups. Learning IS frequently social.*

> MENTORING/SHADOWING: *for those learner outcomes best learned with the aid of a real-world practitioner in a close mentor/mentee relationship.*

INFORMAL LEARNING GROUPS: *for those more mature students who choose to work together to support each other as they work through online learning outcomes.*

About Categorizing Learner Outcomes

The final step to complete this component of the infrastructure required to "roll out" **MCL** is to code or categorize each enabling learner outcome with the "how best learned" strategies. For some learner outcomes, there will be an obvious *best learned* strategy, for others there may be two or more. The learner needs to know how each learner outcome is best learned, and the system needs to know that as well so that they can design appropriate learning opportunities for each outcome.

It is good to remember that a complex vision of this type will have some bumps in its implementation, no matter how complete and diligent the planning. Learner outcomes initially coded with one strategy might have to be placed in another category if the process first chosen is not getting the results we want and need. All effective organizations have "continuous improvement" processes to help them get better and better at what they do. Success is transitory . . . just because you are successful today doesn't mean that you will compete well in the future. Quality is also transitory . . . yesterday's quality is tomorrow's commodity.

The above listing of learning alternatives should not be viewed as THE model, but as an example. Your in-house professionals may choose different labels and different learning experiences. A caution however, the learning experiences that you choose for your **MCL** system must be consistent with the ten *Babies* that we did not throw out with the *Bathwater* in Chapter 5. In other words, the learning opportunities you identify must be true to what we know about learners and learning, and about teachers and teaching. And a second caution, just because a teaching technique worked well in the Industrial Age assembly line school, where you worked with twenty-eight fifteen-year olds taking English I, does not mean that it is also appropriate in a **MCL** system.

4. The School System Has Created and Placed Online Learner Outcomes Online

Think . . . iTunes and their inventory of millions of songs that can be identified, downloaded, played, and paid for from anywhere, at any time.

The surveys that we have taken when working with groups of educators, including teachers, indicate that experienced educators think that more than fifty percent of what we now expect learners to learn could be learned as well or better via technology . . . computers and online learning. Middle school and high school teachers go higher. Some as high as seventy percent.

We continue to make this statement, but we want to be very clear. **MCL** is not cyber schools. We believe that **MCL** actually professionalizes what teachers do. If we can teach fifty percent or more via technology, we have freed our professional teachers to teach the most important things that are best learned with the aid of a talented professional. However, when labeling each enabling learner outcome with the most appropriate learning format, it is much more efficient and effective if we can get as many outcomes into the "online" category as possible. Doing so leaves the professional with smaller groups of learners where personalizing learning requires a personal touch, at the elbow feedback, coaching, encouraging "atta girls" and "atta boys."

In brief then, this infrastructure component requires that the professionals in the system . . . including curriculum, instruction, assessment, and instructional technology experts . . . create online learning opportunities for each learner outcome identified as an outcome that can be "best learned" via technology.

We certainly don't believe that you have to start from scratch in creating these technology-driven learning opportunities . . . what a daunting task that would be. Much good work has already been done in this regard, and the quality and quantity of online learning is increasing dramatically by the week. More than creators, we must be seekers, assessors, field testers, adaptors, and adopters. Stealers? Borrowers? We need to get it where we can. We like to joke when working with groups that when you steal from one person it's called plagiarism . . . but when you steal from everyone, it's called research. Kidding aside, we need to act professionally as we look for online learning resources, but we have to begin with an assumption that there are a great deal of online learning resources available and we don't have to create it all ourselves.

So when this infrastructure component is "ready for rollout," each learner outcome to be learned via technology will be available 24/7 online to all with a need to learn.

5. The School System Has Created Seminars for Learner Outcomes Requiring an Interactive Seminar Format

Think . . . how our best universities do it now.

"Seminar" is the label that we have chosen to give those learning experiences that require learner to teacher, and learner to learner interaction. You may wish to give them a different label, but whatever the label, this teaching and learning format is destined to be a significant part of the learning process. It is in this format that many of the important, somewhat subjective, and critical outcomes are studied, experienced, and learned . . . and it is the format in which the professional teacher shines. Shines by applying many of the professional teaching strategies, the *"Babies"* if you would, that are listed and described in Chapter 5.

The way we envision seminars is quite similar to the manner in which university classes are designed, and similar to the manner in which their availability is communicated to college students. Seminars are designed around specific learner outcomes identified in the Strategic Design process and the subsequent curriculum development that identifies important "enabling learner outcomes." Each seminar can be easily traced to one or more general learner outcomes in one or more Spheres of Living. (See Chapter 3) Learners readily see how each seminar relates to life after they leave school.

At a minimum, written descriptions of each seminar will include:

Seminar Outcome(s):	*a clear statement of what learners will demonstrate to show mastery of intended learnings.*
Seminar Description:	*a two or three paragraph description of the content, the format, and the scheduling scheme of the seminar.*
Learning Facilitators:	*the names of the professionals who will conduct the seminars and maybe a note or two about their qualifications.*
Prerequisites:	*the online learner outcomes and the seminars that must be completed prior to admission to the seminar, as well as any readings or viewings required for entry.*
Scheduling Opportunities:	*the number of classroom hours, how the hours are divided into learning chunks, and the different times the seminar will be available throughout the year.*
Location:	*where the seminar will be conducted.*
Misc:	*any other information pertinent to this specific seminar.*

Students and their learning coaches must be able to schedule these seminars online from anywhere and at any time. A big order, even in this day of customizing technology . . . but the technology to do it is available now and is being used successfully in many business and industries. The following is what the scheduling technology must accommodate to be "ready for rollout:"

☑ The schedule of all seminars, including all of the data about each seminar as listed above is available through a link on the school system's home page. Everyone has access to all seminar information.

☑ The scheduling technology that allows a learner:
  - to register for a seminar,
  - to be informed if there is space available for that particular seminar,
  - to be informed about other seminar opportunities available if there is no room available in the requested seminar,
  - to automatically inform seminar facilitators of the learner's registration, and
  - to signal seminar facilitators to invite the new registrant and to inform him/her of any particulars for this specific seminar.

☑ A system that allows learning facilitators to inform everyone with the need to know if the learner has or has not completed the seminar successfully, and automatically updates the learner's electronic portfolio – including any electronic media of the student demonstrating the learner outcome(s) of the seminar.

(A realization as we were writing this section . . . this is almost exactly the same technology that more than one hundred Phoenix, AZ golf courses use to schedule tee times online. A listing of tee times, including flexible fees dependent upon time of day and day of week updated daily, includes credit card payment, all friction free, prints out our receipts and registrations, tells us no denim is allowed and that shirts with collars are required. . . still amazes us how they know that we're from South Dakota or Maine!)

6. The School System Has Designed and Implemented Scheduling Technology for Individual Learners

Think . . . Microsoft or Yahoo! Calendars
and how individuals and work teams schedule their activities.

In Chapter 7, "*Lori Does Her Learning Schedule,*" you were able to see scheduling from a learner's perspective. If customized learner scheduling is to happen as smoothly as it appeared when Lori did it, what infrastructure did the IT people have to provide to make the process so seamless and friction free? What IT must do to have the scheduling technology "ready for rollout:"

☑ The school system should identify the most effective electronic scheduling technology available and make one specific scheduling calendar uniform throughout the system.

☑ The school system must have a master calendar (most school systems do this now) that includes all extracurricular activities   to include practice schedules as well as events.

☑ Each learner outcome, including online learning outcomes, should be numerically coded to make it easy to enter into the small space of the scheduling calendar.

☑ The scheduling system must ensure that only those with a "need to know" are able to access the schedule or the records of individual learners.

7. The School System Has Designed and Implemented "Accountability Technology" for Administration

*Think . . .Walmart and its ability to track individual products
from their manufacturer to the purchasing consumer.*

Accountability can take many forms. For school systems, we typically think "accountability for student learning" when we hear or use that term. But from a principal's perspective....and certainly from a parent's perspective....the first line of school system accountability is "where is Lori and is she safe." Once we know that our learners are being cared for in safe surroundings, we want learning to happen, but there is little doubt about top priority.

MCL creates a concern in this regard, especially when compared to and contrasted with our bureaucratic assembly line schools of today. One good thing we can say about the Industrial Age ....we knew where everyone was supposed to be. When a call came to the principal's office from Lori's Mom, we knew that Lori was a sophomore, it's 10:15, third period, she is in Ms. Trezona's English II class, and Trezona teaches in #204....I can walk down the hall and give Lori the message.

If we want to have **MCL** accepted by parents, it is essential that we show that we can be flexible, meet individual learner needs and schedules while simultaneously tracking, supervising, and protecting all learners. Being "ready for rollout" means that we must:

▶ Create a tracking system that allows school leaders/principals to quickly determine where each student is located and how he/she can be contacted. This will require that every learner's schedule include the location of their learning activity at all times during each day. (Walmart does this now with each of their products. General Motors does this with automobiles by applying their OnStar program.)

▶ Those with a "need to know" (parents, learning coach, school principal or representative) the location of a student at any time will have access to that information via a secure password.

▶ Those with "a need to know" will have access to that specific learner's electronic portfolio which will inform parents, learning coach, and special counselors of individual learner progress. Technology also allows those with "a need to know" to be informed of that specific learner's achievement in comparison to school system norms. Many other comparisons could be made given the speed and power of today's technology. For instance, the system could track how a specific learner is achieving as compared to the college or university of his/her choice; how the learner compares to girls and/or boys of his/her own age.

This list could continue but we think you get the point. Feedback loops that effectively foster the "continuous improvement" of individuals and organizations can be designed around almost any goal. All we need do is decide

- what is important to improve,

- what data needs to be collected to determine progress,

- how that data will be collected, and

- how we will use that data to make decisions about how to improve our processes.

We can decide that for which we hold school systems accountable.

Technology of today, and that of tomorrow, allows us to keep detailed records of almost anything and make almost any type of comparisons. But just because it can be done doesn't mean that it should be done. Individual parents and local school systems will have to make value-based decisions regarding how technology will be used.

Making It Happen . . . the Superintendent Starts the MCL Ball Rolling

This may be a good time to discuss who should be doing all of this. The short answer is: the implementation of the **MCL** vision is everyone's job, everyone's job description, everyone's reason for being employed by the system. Visionary leaders need to ensure that everyone . . . and that means EVERYONE. . . must understand how the **MCL** vision will impact their work. Only then can they become contributors.

Although the previous statement is very true, very right, and must be ingrained throughout the system, we suggest a starting point that is more specific. The morning after the Board meeting at which the Board approved the Strategic Design for the school system, the Superintendent should call a meeting of his/her leadership team. Included on this team ~~should~~ must be all Assistant Superintendents, Directors of Curriculum, Instruction, Student Assessment, Directors of Technology, the Business Manager, and the person responsible for auxiliary services. The structure and titles of your organization may differ from these, but it is the roles that people play that is important. Basically, anyone who has leadership responsibilities for anything having to do with curriculum, instruction, student assessment, technology, the budget, and with support services should be at the meeting.

The meeting should be informal but certainly with a clear agenda. We suggest that the superintendent be forceful and clear about the purpose of the meeting and, more importantly, about his/her total commitment to the **MCL** vision. Somewhere in this two- to four-hour meeting, it should become clear to everyone that the new vision is not option-

...the new vision is not optional

al. Somewhere during this meeting everyone should become aware of his/her personal fit with the direction the system is taking. *"Am I excited about this vision, does it fit my values, my skills? Do I have the energy? Can I do it? Do I really want to be part of it? What scares me? Is this good for me, my career?"*

We believe that the superintendent should be candid about the fact that the new vision may not be right for everyone and that this might be the time for each of us/them to make the basic decision — should I stay or should I go. This may seem harsh and uncaring, but it is not. What is harsh and uncaring is to put people into positions that don't sync with their values, abilities, and career plans, to put people into positions that may make it difficult for the organization to realize its learner-focused vision. School systems are not in the employment business, they are in the student learning business.

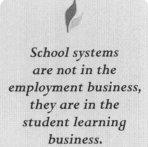

School systems are not in the employment business, they are in the student learning business.

The focus of this very important meeting should be the **MCL** vision and the team effort required to make that vision a reality. The vision . . . everyone should be very familiar with the new vision. They were part of its creation, they have since talked about it with their colleagues, they have asked questions and they have had ample opportunities to reflect on their role in making the vision a reality. They have probably already made their "to go" or "to stay" decision . . . and hopefully that decision was an enthusiastic "I want to be part of this!"

Ensuring that the leadership "group" becomes a leadership "team" ~~may be~~ - WILL BE - a bit more problematic. Our traditional, Industrial Age school structure allows and supports each office, each department acting and functioning as a single unit. The curriculum office does curriculum, the assessment people handle the testing program, the business manager creates and manages the budget, and the superintendent "takes care of the board." Bureaucracies function like that. You do your job, I do mine; if we all do what our office was designed to do, the system will run smoothly. Bureaucracies have departments that function as "silos" and are managed. Today's effective customer-centered organizations require "networks" that

Moving people from managers of silos to members of a vision-driven team is the task of the effective CEO.

function as teams and are led. Moving people from managers of silos to members of a vision-driven team is the task of the effective CEO. Today's complex problems are seldom solved by one person or one department. Making **MCL** a reality requires talented people committed to a team effort. Everyone should leave this meeting committed to functioning as a team and thinking about how they will relay this same message to their team:

> *"The next leadership team meeting . . . and it will be soon, so clear calendars . . . will be for the purpose of creating a concrete plan for the team to address the seven* **MCL** *infrastructure requirements."*

Vision Ambassadors

Creating meaningful organizational change is difficult. Creating meaningful change in schools is VERY difficult. We will need all the help we can get. Everyone knows education, they have been there, been there a long time, have not seen schools change in any meaningful way in their entire lifetime, and that makes it doubly hard for us to think outside-the-box. The experts we have heard from tell us that community members listen to, and believe most, those things they hear from their children and from support staff employees.

Community members in conversation at the vegetable counter at Safeway more quickly accept the descriptions and opinions of teacher aides regarding the school system than those of principals, and the superintendent's secretary is more believable than the superintendent. At first, this doesn't sound very plausible, but then we think of how quickly we believe Walmart checkers when we ask them "What's it like to work at Walmart?" and how on-guard and skeptical we would be if we asked that same question of the store manager.

With that in mind, how can we use . . . maybe "use" is not the right word . . . make that . . . how can we elicit the support of our learners and our staff in communicating and gaining support for our **MCL** vision? How can we help them to become ambassadors for our vision, for this meaningful change with such a great deal of potential? First step would seem to be ensuring that <u>all</u> learners and <u>all</u> staff members are able to enthusiastically articulate the critical aspects of the **MCL** vision and are quick to list its benefits. "Wiifys" – "what's in it for you" as labeled in the "change" literature. Benefits not just for learners, but for everyone. Not least of which is giving taxpayers a big, big bang for their buck. (Wish we had time and space to explain that.)

More about leadership and the change process in the following chapter that we have titled "*Total Leaders.*"

Chapter 9
Takeaways:

Being "ready for rollout" requires that all **MCL** infrastructure components be in place, that the system has been tested and proven to work smoothly, and that everyone knows the new MOs.

Involving everyone in the change process is critical to gaining commitment for the change and to ensuring a smooth/healthy/effective "rollout.

In the end, **MCL** will happen if everyone . . . all constituencies, want it to happen.

*"Information technology and business are inextricably interwoven.
I don't think that anyone can talk meaningfully about
one without talking about the other."*

Bill Gates

*If you always do what you've always done,
You'll always get what you've always got.*

Total Leaders

"What would you do if you weren't afraid?"

Debbie Millman

"If you're big enough to dream,
Your dream isn't big enough for you."

Erwin Raphael McManus

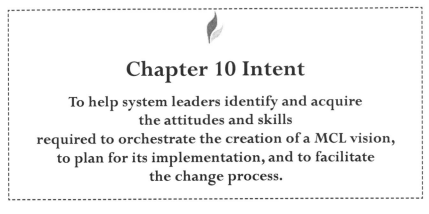

Chapter 10 Intent

**To help system leaders identify and acquire
the attitudes and skills
required to orchestrate the creation of a MCL vision,
to plan for its implementation, and to facilitate
the change process.**

After an introduction to Total Leaders, we will apply the Total Leaders Framework to the planning for, and implementation of, MASS CUSTOMIZED LEARNING. We will give you our best advice on how you can apply the best leadership thinking to the exciting **MCL** vision.

Total Leaders: A Short History

In 1998 Charles Schwahn and William Spady were asked to write *Total Leaders: Applying the Best Future-Focused Change Strategies to Education* for the American Association of School Administrators. The book was based on what has become known as the "Total Leaders Framework." The framework and the book became very popular, and in 2010 Schwahn and Spady were asked to write a second edition that is titled *Total Leaders 2.0: Leading in the Age of Empowerment*. This chapter is about applying the Total Leaders Framework to the MASS CUSTOMIZED LEARNING vision.

The title *Total Leaders* is quite descriptive of the book and framework. Schwahn and Spady's leadership work is based on a synthesis of today's leading leadership and change gurus, and on more than one hundred of the most popular leadership books of the recent past. The framework answers the question:

> *If Covey, Peters, Blanchard, Bennis, Senge, Wheatley, Maxwell, Buckingham, Drucker, etc. etc., were in one room and asked, 'What about leadership would all of you agree upon?' the answer would be the Total Leaders Framework.*

Stated in a less grandiose but self-serving manner, Schwahn and Spady have stolen everything they know about leadership from the people who DO.

TL 2.0: The Short Course

Your understanding of the TL2.0 framework will be enhanced if you now and then take a peek at the two diagrams that follow. The first diagram is linear and includes the Strategic Design aspects of leadership and management. The second diagram is spatial . . . the position of each leadership domain to the other domains has significance. Authentic Leadership is the central domain and is at the "heart" of the model.

This first diagram starts the explanation of Total Leaders with Strategic Design, the place where big picture leadership begins. Leadership 101 divides Strategic Design into two parts.

> *Setting a Strategic Direction* typically includes the organization's core values, its mission (in the case of school systems, exit learner outcomes), and the vision of what the organization will look like when it is operating at its ideal best.

> *Strategic Alignment* is about aligning all aspects of the organization with its vision, and typically includes aligning its people, policies, processes, and organizational structure with that vision.

In short, Leadership 101 identifies the leader's broad responsibility for 1) setting the organization's direction, and 2) creating the organizational alignment that will effectively move the organization in that direction. The very bottom of the diagram identifies the successful results of these responsibilities: *Total Leaders Creating Productive Change.*

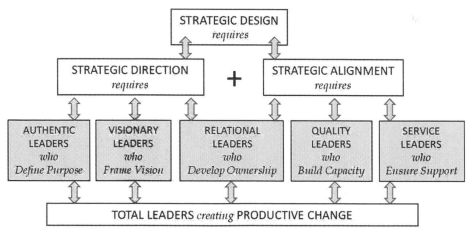

Five Leadership Domains and Five Pillars of Change

But in between Strategic Design and successful productive change results, *there is leadership.* We (Schwahn and Spady), based on the insights of the leadership and change gurus from whom we learn, divide leadership into five essential Leadership Domains and five critical Pillars of Change (Purpose, Vision, Ownership, Capacity, Support).

AUTHENTIC LEADERS
> *who create a compelling organizational purpose and a reason to change. (PURPOSE)*

VISIONARY LEADERS
> *who describe a concrete picture of the change…and help everyone understand how the change will affect him/her personally. (VISION)*

RELATIONAL LEADERS
> *who involve everyone in the change process . . . and create commitment to the change. (OWNERSHIP)*

QUALITY LEADERS
> *who develop and empower everyone . . . and create the capacity to change. (CAPACITY)*

SERVICE LEADERS
> *who manage the vision . . . and provide support for the change. (SUPPORT)*

The second diagram of the Total Leaders Framework portrays the Leadership Domains in a relational and interactive manner. Note that the Authentic Leader is at the heart of this model, for without the presence of an authentic leader influencing all other domains, meaningful change will be difficult if not impossible.

KEY DOMAINS OF TOTAL LEADERS

You can now put together Strategic Design, the Leadership Domains, and the Pillars of Change and you will see why one might expect Productive Change as a result. *Inevitable: Mass Customized Learning* simply asks you, the leader, to plug **MCL** into the vision piece, and the Productive Change that the Total Leaders Framework will produce will be a **MCL** learning system.

Performance Roles of the Total Leader

The Total Leaders 2.0 Framework becomes more concrete and user friendly when we add the Performance Roles to each Leadership Domain. The Performance Roles answer the question:

> *What do Authentic Leaders actually do?*
> *What do Visionary Leaders actually do?* and so forth.

We will provide a quick listing of the three most critical Performance Roles for each Leadership Domain and Change Pillar here, and then spend much of the remainder of this chapter describing how these roles can/will/must be applied if a **MCL** vision is to become reality.

These Performance Roles have been identified through a thorough study of more than one hundred of the best-selling leadership and change books of recent years. We asked ourselves:

> *What does this guru tell us about what successful leaders actually do? Beyond theory and personality, what are the activities of the successful leader?*

The identification of the five Leadership Domains actually became part of the leadership model after the Performance Domains had been identified. The Total Leaders Framework is not a top down model, but rather a bottom up model. We expect that you will believe and trust it all, but if you want our take on the credibility of the model, it begins with the Performance Roles.

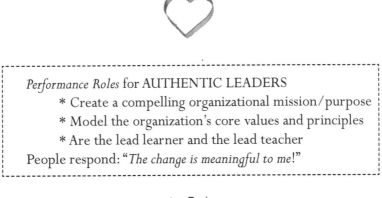

Performance Roles for AUTHENTIC LEADERS
    * Create a compelling organizational mission/purpose
    * Model the organization's core values and principles
    * Are the lead learner and the lead teacher
People respond: "*The change is meaningful to me!*"

Performance Roles for VISIONARY LEADERS
    * Define an ideal future for their organization
    * Consistently employ a client/student focus
    * Expand organizational options
People respond: "*Our direction is exciting!*"

Performance Roles for RELATIONAL LEADERS
    * Develop a change-friendly culture
    * Involve everyone in the change process
    * Create meaning for everyone
People respond: "*I want to be part of the change!*"

Performance Roles for QUALITY LEADERS
* Develop and empower everyone
* Create and use feedback loops
* Improve organizational performance
People respond: "*I can do that!*"

Performance Roles for SERVICE LEADERS
* Manage the organization's vision
* Restructure the organization to achieve results
* Reward positive contributions
People respond: "*Our leaders are helping us do it!*"

Performance Roles (PR) Applied

This section will tie the Total Leaders Framework to the **MCL** vision. The "to do" part of each Performance Role is presented in a linear fashion so as to be easily understood; however, those of you with leadership experience will quickly realize that real systemic change efforts are not quite this neat and tidy. (Note: The PRs will be described from the leader's point of view.)

AUTHENTIC LEADERSHIP DOMAIN
Creating the reason to change

Performance Role # 1: *Creating a Compelling Organization Mission / Purpose*

Chapter 3, "*But First . . . Our Purpose,*" details the essential components of Strategic Design and Strategic Direction. The direction setting essentials, the "what" part of the process, include core organizational values, organizational mission, and exit learner outcomes. Chapter 3 provides examples. The following "how to" part of the direction setting process has been learned from our leadership gurus as well as from our firsthand experiences.

▶ Creating a compelling purpose does not begin when you have 120 people in one room who represent all important role groups and you are introducing the strategic design process. It begins with your study of the future, your cross-industry learning, and the resultant vision for meaningful change that you create. (Interesting, but after clicking this last sentence, we realized that in a general sense this is just the way the **MCL** vision came to be . . . for us.)

When you initially come upon your vision, it will probably be very sketchy. And that is good, because when you begin to share that sketchy vision, you will find that others have ideas that make the vision more complete. Grab this opportunity to begin using "we" rather than "I" when you next describe the enhanced vision. Enough of these exchanges and you will have a good start in gaining the commitment you will need to sell the vision to the organization and to the community.

We suggest that you talk with everyone who will listen about the **MCL** vision, but put special emphasis on gaining the understanding and support of the Board of Education and the Leadership Team.

▶ You may want an outside facilitator to facilitate the Strategic Direction process, but if you do, scout the facilitator as he/she works through the process for someone else and make sure that he/she understands your vision and your expectations for the process. Know and remember that writing is not a group task. Gaining consensus regarding direction *is* a group task, but putting those decisions in written form is best when done by not more than three people . . . and you should be one of those three. We hesitate to do this, but you might want to contact either Chuck or Bea as you design your strategic direction setting process. We are not looking for business but we will share good examples of school systems that have done it well. Be careful to get this part right; everything else you do will depend on this basic Strategic Design work. We are reminded (from our respective home construction experiences) of the importance of getting the frame of the building square . . . or else you will fight sloppy angles for the rest of the project.

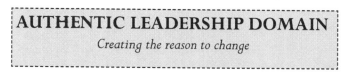

AUTHENTIC LEADERSHIP DOMAIN
Creating the reason to change

Performance Role # 2: *Modeling the Organization's Core Values and Principles*

Before one can model core values and principles, one must have identified them. We again suggest the advice of Stephen Covey, "If it's important, it should be intentional," and the moral foundations of the leader and the organization ARE important. The lists of values and principles that follow are those most frequently found in the leadership and change literature. Some are old standbys and some have been made relevant by the speed of today's world and our new technologies.

(Note: Definitions for each of these core values and principles of professionalism, along with the process for creating your organization's moral foundation can be found in Schwahn and Spady's *Total Leaders 2.0: Leading in the Age of Empowerment* published by the American Association of School Administrators and Rowman and Littlefield Press, 2010.)

Principles of professionalism are those ethical standards of decision making and performance that transcend personal considerations and circumstantial pressures to promote the higher good of the organization and its clients.

Universal Core Organizational Values

Integrity	*Courage*	*Honesty*	*Reflection*	*Commitment*
Productivity	*Teamwork*	*Openness*	*Excellence*	*Risk taking*

Principles of Professionalism

Inquiry	*Alignment*	*Improvement*	*Contribution*	*Accountability*
Clarity	*Win-Win*	*Inclusiveness*	*Connection*	*Future-Focusing*

Although all of these values and principles are important, we suggest that leaders and leadership teams identify two or three from each list upon which to focus. For instance, those values most aligned with **MCL** might be courage, commitment, and risk taking, and those principles might be future-focusing, improvement, and inclusiveness.

Integrity of course is core value number 1 for leaders. We most often hear integrity defined as "walking your talk." And walking the talk IS critical to the Authentic Leader. But equally important for the leader is "talking their walk." Modeling is most influential when others are aware of what you are modeling. And if you want the entire staff and community to embrace those critical values and principles, it's good to let people know when you are doing it. Instead of simply making a statement that is value-laden, the leader might introduce the statement by prefacing it with "Given that we value *honesty,* I think it's important that we are open with the Board and the community about . . . ."

Leaders "model" at all times. People watch leaders . . . and they interpret your words, actions, and decisions. If they like you, their interpretations tend to be positive. If they don't like you, they tend to see things you do as negative and/ or manipulative. So be a good guy/good gal without being a phony.

Remember that you are always on stage whether you like it or not; the staff and community put you there. Where you go and what you do are meaningful in many ways. Saying you are very supportive of the music program is not as believable as is your attendance at the music concert. You can pretend to care, but you can't pretend to be there.

When you walk that talk,
you reveal the ranking of your values.
Alan Deutschman

AUTHENTIC LEADERSHIP DOMAIN
Creating the reason to change

Performance Role # 3: *Being the Lead Learner and the Lead Teacher*

Peter Senge, in his 1990 bestseller *The Fifth Discipline*, created the "learning organization" label that has brought focus to a performance role that has become critical to the Total Leader in the age of rapid change. If the world around your organization is changing faster than your organization, your organization is most likely on its way to becoming obsolete.

> *If the world around your organization is changing faster than your organization, your organization is most likely on its way to becoming obsolete.*

Total Leaders need to be lifelong learners who create learning organizations. Success has become transitory, and staying on top requires that individuals and organizations learn from what is happening outside their organization, as well as from what is happening inside their organization. Learning organizations are quick to share information throughout the system. They watch the horizon and study the future, they create feedback loops and gather data from within, and they are eager to share those learnings with everyone.

Educational lead learners are open to "cross-industry learning" and find ways to apply the mass customizing technologies of Apple, Inc., Amazon.com, Wikipedia, etc. to the delivery of instruction in schools. Lead learners learn what other organizations are doing that might be transferable to education, and then they ask themselves and their people, "How do they do that?" and "How might we use that to better serve learner needs?" The **MCL** vision is the result of this watching, learning, and transfer process.

People and organizations are changed when leaders are able to articulate a convincing philosophy and rationale for change. Most paradigm changing visions begin with general ideas and possibilities and become more defined and comprehensive with study, reflection, and discussion. At this point, the **MCL** vision is quite complete . . . complete with a philosophy, a rationale, and the basic "how tos" of implementation. The lead learner/teacher must be able to "teach" the vision to his/her leadership team, staff, and community.

So be ready with that ninety-second elevator explanation of **MCL**, that ten-minute persuasive talk for the Chamber of Commerce luncheon, and for that question-and-answer session that you will be holding at each of your schools. That idea you had about a weekly column on the topic is a good one . . . and by the way, can you convince your staff and community of the need to support an in-depth Strategic Design process? You got into this business because of your love of learning and teaching, right? Well this just might be your greatest opportunity! Go for it! Enjoy it!

VISIONARY LEADERSHIP DOMAIN

Painting a Concrete Picture of the Change

Performance Role # 4: *Defining an Ideal Future for Your Organization*

This entire book is about creating a vision . . . a MASS CUSTOMIZED LEARNING vision. The **MCL** vision was a focus of Chapter 4, *"Through the Learner's Eyes,"* Chapter 6, *"**MCL**: The Vision,"* and Chapter 7, *"Lori Does Her Learning Schedule."*

So we will assume that you now understand the Total Leader's role in creating, communicating, and "selling" the **MCL** vision . . . or any vision of your choice for that matter. But allow us, as a review, to make a few statements about the critical "*Defining an ideal future for your organization*" performance role. (Performance Role #13, described later, is about *Managing* the Organization's Vision.)

▶ Warren Bennis suggested that bold visions, much like masterpiece paintings, are not created by committee but are the result of one person's insight and creativity. And that person just may not be you but one of your team members. No matter from whence the vision comes, work quickly to make it *our* vision rather than *my* vision.

▶ There are new visions that strike from out of the blue, but there is a better chance that they will come from an innovation already proven successful in another business or industry . . . be watchful for "cross-industry learning" opportunities.

▶ The **MCL** vision described in *Inevitable* should be viewed as *one way* to customize learning for every learner. Your vision may be different and maybe even better. But be careful, any vision that retains the assembly line delivery of instruction negates the potential for MASS CUSTOMIZED LEARNING.

▶ New visions, to be meaningful and powerful, must run well ahead of your present capacity to implement them. Impactful visions *pull* people and organizations into a new future. If your idea is a good thing and you already have the capacity to do it, get on with it . . . but call it a "goal" and not a vision.

▶ Everyone must understand how the new vision will impact his/her role and contributions to the organization. Bus drivers and office secretaries and everyone else will be significantly impacted by the **MCL** vision.

VISIONARY LEADERSHIP DOMAIN
Painting a Concrete Picture of the Change

Performance Role # 5: *Consistently Employing a Client/Student Focus*

Does your organization focus on policies, practices, and structures and expect the customer/client to conform? (Think getting your driver's license.) Or does your organization focus on the customer/client and create policies, practices, and structures that meet their needs and desires? (Think Starbucks.)

Traditional school structures are set, and have been for more than one hundred years. If you are a first grader, you will be put in a group of five- or six-year olds and taught how to read . . . ready or not. **MCL** asks the question, "What is Stephanie ready for?" And the answer may be "chapter books," or it may be "speaking and listening vocabulary development."

If kids could vote, we believe that schools would be less bureaucratic and much more customer/learner centered. Seniors vote in high percentages, politicians listen, and they get price breaks (also known as geezer discounts) everywhere.

VISIONARY LEADERSHIP DOMAIN
Painting a Concrete Picture of the Change

Performance Role # 6: *Expanding Organizational Options*

If visionary leaders can replace the weight bearing walls described in Chapter 8 and replace them with today's customizing technologies, the gates can be opened to unlimited options. Rather than to have leaders say "that's a great idea, but how can we do it when we have a rigid grade level structure and a rigid student grouping system," they would be able to say, "what a great idea, how do you think we should do it?" And after hearing the teacher's idea, respond with, "what can I do, or stop doing to make it easy for you implement your vision?"

We don't want to sound too Pollyannaish, as we realize how hard it is to change education. Educators and parents have institutionalized and internalized our bureaucratic Industrial Age structure making it nearly impossible to think outside of our educational boxes. But the good news is that, until now, we didn't have living proof that there are ways to mass customize learning. There didn't seem to be a choice, there didn't seem to be organizational options, but now there are. Visionary leaders need to trust that when people understand the desirability of **MCL**, and also recognize that the means now exist to make it a reality, they will see the value in options that allow educators to implement our most basic research regarding motivation and learning.

Trust . . . that if educators are given the opportunity to become more professional, they will do it! Trust . . . that if parents learn of a system that will meet the individual needs of their children, they will want it. In time, they will demand it. It's *Inevitable!*

RELATIONAL LEADERSHIP DOMAIN
Gaining Commitment for the Change

Performance Role # 7: *Creating a Change-friendly Culture*

Change is a major definer of today's world . . . and especially the definer of today's successful businesses and organizations. Change to meet today's demands as perceived by the customers/clients, or get run over by those who do. That's today's reality, a reality that runs up against a most common human trait . . . we don't want to change. Change messes with our beliefs, our routines and our security. When we talk of "necessary change," we are usually talking about "what those other people should be doing differently and better."

The relational leader is a cultural leader. She knows that organizational cultures silently let everyone in the organization know what is OK to do, and what is not OK to do. Differing cultures have differing "dos" and "don'ts." Google values and rewards innovation, but their accounting department probably does not. FedEx thinks "customer satisfaction, innovation, and improvement" and rewards it. The US Postal service thinks "policies, rules, and stability," and rewards it. Guess which is consistently improving its services . . . while making a profit?

The cultural leader is aware that being change friendly is about thinking outside the box, about innovation, and about risk taking. She also knows firsthand that we eventually get the attitudes and behaviors that we reward, and we extinguish those behaviors that we don't reward. She knows that change-friendly attitudes and behaviors must be encouraged, supported, and rewarded.

RELATIONAL LEADERSHIP DOMAIN
Gaining Commitment for the Change

Performance Role # 8: *Involving Everyone in the Change Process*

There are many good reasons for involving people in the change process. The first that usually comes to mind is that by involving people we gain their commitment to the change, which smoothes the way for implementation. Fine and good, but if that's the basic reason we involve people, we may be manipulating more than leading. Total Leaders believe that involving people will promote better decisions. They believe that people will have good ideas about what should be done and how it should be done. They believe that "no one of us is as smart as all of us." They believe in _The Wisdom of Crowds_.

There is another powerful and sometimes overlooked reason for involving people in decisions that will affect them. When people are involved in discussions they learn about the issues, the decisions, and the rationale behind the decisions. When they know and believe, they become advocates for the change and help to sell the idea to others. In short, involving people in the change process is a great way of communicating the change throughout the organization and the community. Change is much easier to sell when leaders spend the time up-front in the change process rather than to try to sell an idea that was made in private or by a small powerful group.

Relational leaders are good listeners and demonstrate their trust in people from day one. They know that all decisions can't be made by consensus lest the organization get bogged down in process, but they know those decisions that are emotional in nature should involve those who will be impacted. The big issues, like Strategic Design, obviously require heavy involvement from all constituencies. Chapter 3, "But First . . . Our Purpose" describes how the relational leader involves people in the rather complex direction setting process. The time it takes to involve everyone and to do it right will pay off when the "heavy lifting" required to make the **MCL** vision a reality begins.

RELATIONAL LEADERSHIP DOMAIN
Gaining Commitment for the Change

Performance Role # 9: _Creating Meaning for Everyone_

Yesterday it seemed enough for people to have a good job, to be able to pay their bills, to retire at sixty-five and begin doing the things that were fun and interesting. But for a large percentage of today's workers/employees, that's not enough. Today we want our work to be interesting, challenging, and meaningful. We want to lead _A Purposeful Life_, and that includes our work life. The relational leader embraces this expectation.

Some jobs and roles are quite naturally meaningful. Some are not. From our (Bea and Chuck) point of view, no work, no role, is more meaningful than preparing young people to succeed in the world they will encounter after they leave school. So "creating meaning for everyone" is a natural for the educational leader. Even for those not directly involved in the teaching/learning process. Do bus drivers get students to school safely, or might their role be defined as "getting children to school ready to learn?" Do custodians clean up after kids, or do they work with teachers and learners to "create a positive learning environment?" The work activities may appear to be the same, but the mind-set, the motivation, the reality, and the meaningfulness of the work are very different. Of course the leader has to believe deeply that getting children to school ready to learn is a significant contribution to the learning process, that custodians really do influence the child's learning.

Meaningful work is a powerful intrinsic motivator. Studies confirm that people who find meaning in their work are engaged, need little supervision, and are significantly more productive than those who see their work as "just a job." Relational leaders consciously and intentionally help everyone to find meaning in their work. Could anything be more meaningful than the successful implementation of the **MCL** vision!

QUALITY LEADERSHIP DOMAIN
Creating the Capacity to Change

Performance Role # 10: *Developing and Empowering Everyone*

We live in an age of empowerment . . . empowerment defined as "people being in control of the variables they deem important to their success." Most people today desire and at times demand that they have control of what they do and how they do it. They want their work to be a clear reflection of their values, talents, and passions. And it's all a good thing, a big win-win. Employees find meaning in the work they do, and leaders have learned that empowered people produce . . . and what they produce is typically high quality. Businesses today find it difficult to compete without consciously and intentionally empowering individuals and teams.

Given the positive aspects of empowerment, quality leaders don't leave empowerment to chance. They hire for it, create expectations that everyone will be empowered, and develop those not yet ready to be empowered.

Staff development, once thought to be the responsibility of the organization, is now a shared responsibility. Individuals are expected to be continuous learners who keep themselves up-to-date, and organizations are expected to provide training on those processes and skills unique to the organization's operation. People change jobs and careers much more often today than in the past and the term "jobless security" has come to mean that although the organization may no longer need you, you are "sooo with the latest" that you will have another position by Monday.

Education is a people oriented business/profession. Operating a quality school system obviously requires quality people. **MCL** requires people who are dedicated, talented, empowered, innovative, and not afraid to take well-thought-out risks. The general structure and operation of a **MCL** system is quite clear, but the day-to-day operational glue necessary to hold it all together needs to be created. Empowered educators will find joy in making the **MCL** vision a reality. This may sound trite, but our experience indicates that educators love young learners, love their work, and find deep meaning in meeting the learning needs of children and young adults. If there is a better way to do that, they will be on board. **MCL** is a better way of doing that.

QUALITY LEADERSHIP DOMAIN
Creating the Capacity to Change

Performance Role # 11: *Creating and Using Feedback Loops*

Performance Role # 12: *Improving Organizational Performance*

These two performance roles are closely related. Quality leaders create and use feedback loops so that they can systematically and continuously improve organizational performance. Although the continuous improvement process is very logical and rather easily explained, its implementation and use can become rather complex and time-consuming . . . but all well worth it.

Total quality management (TQM) was made popular by W. Edwards Deming, an American who, after World War II, helped the Japanese rebuild their productive capacity while introducing the world to the quality paradigm. Basically, TQM and the continuous-improvement process consist of creating and using feedback loops to continuously improve performance. The steps required to accomplish continuous progress include:

1. Identifying your product or service.
   What is it that your organization intends to accomplish? For **MCL** systems the first answer to that question is "student learning." Student

learning defined by the exit learner outcomes that were identified in the Strategic Design process and further defined through the curriculum development process. (See Chapter 3, *"But First....Our Purpose"*)

2. <u>Setting quality standards for your product or services.</u>
   MCL is learner outcome based. What the learner must do to demonstrate his/her learning is written into each learner outcome. When students can demonstrate that learning, they are given credit for it and the demonstration of that learning becomes part of their learner portfolio. If the learner is not able to demonstrate the outcome based upon set standards, the learner isn't finished yet.

3. <u>Identifying the data needed to measure and track your product or service.</u>
   For a **MCL** system based on clearly written learner outcomes, the data to be collected is clear. We want to know how each learner is doing, what he/she is achieving, and we want to know how we are performing as a system. There will also be other aspects of the organization that we want to measure and monitor such as transportation's effectiveness and efficiency, costs of each system's operation, student acceptance of **MCL**, parent assessment of **MCL**, etc. Feedback loops must be created for each aspect that is deemed to be important. This may be a good opportunity to add that feedback loops and continuous improvement are not only for top leadership. Each function, each department, and each learning center will be expected to apply these same techniques to their operation.

4. <u>Determining how to collect, analyze and communicate data to decision makers.</u>
   Again, this is a step made relatively simple by the fact that **MCL** is an outcome driven system. Each learner has a learning portfolio that is updated with each new achievement. Those with a need to know have 24/7 access to that individual learner portfolio. Technology makes it relatively easy to aggregate individual learner achievement, providing a

total system picture . . . actually, providing many system pictures as the data can be analyzed in many formats.

5. <u>Establishing a process to ensure that the data is being used effectively.</u>
   Feedback loops are only useful if the data they create is used to inform future decisions. This step may appear mundane, but if the leaders of any department or learning center are not "quality and continuous improvement oriented," all is for naught. If the data collected is not being used effectively, it may be a good time to ask ourselves if we are measuring the right things, the important things. Focusing on quality and continuous improvement is not optional to the Total Leader.

6. <u>Continuously improving the effectiveness of the feedback loop and the process of the system.</u>
   This step is why we do the other five. If we are not getting the results we want, we must modify or change our practices and processes. And, even if we are getting the results we want, we will want to consider how our practices and processes can be improved to get even better results. Japanese car manufacturers have used their form of these six steps to continuously improve the quality of their cars and the efficiency of their car building processes. Our learners are not cars and we know that, but continuous improvement values and techniques are easily and aptly applied to learning organizations. The payoff will be big.

SERVICE LEADERSHIP DOMAIN

Providing Support for the Change

Performance Role # 13: *Managing the Organization's Vision*

If everything has been done correctly up to this point, the organizational chart gets stood on its head and the leader is in service to those he/she "supervises." This is where the "heavy lifting" begins. Leaders and staff have had the thrill of identifying a compelling purpose and creating a beautiful vision, everyone is committed to **MCL**, and we are all empowered to do what needs to be done . . . so what do we do now . . . GULP.

Strategic plans don't seem to have the same power in school systems as they have in business. In business, after the new vision has been introduced, people ask themselves, *"What does this mean for me, what will I be expected to do differently?"* Where in school systems, after the new vision has been introduced, people might say to themselves, *"Well, that's an option."* And for a vision as powerful and complex as the **MCL** vision, it cannot be "an option."

The supervision process must focus on the implementation of the vision if it is to be taken seriously and become reality. We suggest that the first question the supervisor ask each time there is an opportunity is,

"Tell me what you are doing to help us implement our **MCL** *vision."*

The supervisor should leave no doubt about expectations for focus and implementation. And when the supervisee states what he/she is doing and planning to do, the second question from the supervisor (the service leader) should be, *"What can I do, or stop doing, to help you get that done?"* When the service leader gets back to her office, the first thing she should do is to begin providing the support that was requested.

Marcus Buckingham, respected leadership author and researcher, tells us that leadership and management are different. Both are important, but different. Leaders identify a common purpose and vision and capitalize on it. In our case, that purpose and vision is **MCL**. Managers identify the strengths of the individuals they supervise, and capitalize on them. Capitalize on them to further the implementation of **MCL**.

Buckingham's research has led him to two strong beliefs that appeal to us (Chuck and Bea). One, good leaders are optimists. Optimists are born optimistic. Optimism cannot be taught. Bottom line, not everyone is destined to be an effective leader. Two, good managers work through the strengths and talents of individuals. They create a work situation where those strengths and talents are easily applied. Good managers don't try to "fix" anyone.

SERVICE LEADERSHIP DOMAIN
Providing Support for the Change

Performance Role # 14: *Restructuring the Organization to Achieve Results*

MCL is a transformational change for education and, as such, demands significantly different organizational structures. The present structure of public schools, with its bureaucratic policies and practices, its Industrial Age assembly line delivery of instruction, and its time based learning opportunities, cannot be morphed into a structure that will support **MCL**. If education is to take advantage of today's transformational technologies to meet the personal and individual learning needs of every learner every day, the structure of learning systems has to be designed with the learner as the first focus. Tinkering with the old system won't cut it. When visions change and structures stay the same, nothing happens. Form (structures) must follow function (educating unique learners) if the system is to be effective and efficient.

The structure required for **MCL** is detailed in chapters seven, eight, and nine. The Industrial Age weight bearing walls identified in Chapter 8 need to be replaced by today's transformational technologies. The new infrastructure requirements described in Chapter 9 must replace the bureaucratic infrastructure of today's outdated school systems. All of this so Lori can schedule her learning activities as suggested in Chapter 7, and have learning days like the one described in Chapter 4. It's all very desirable; it's all very doable. Performance Role # 14, *Restructuring the Organization to Achieve Results* is the hard part . . . but well worth it. It's *Inevitable*.

SERVICE LEADERSHIP DOMAIN
Providing Support for the Change

Performance Role # 15: *Rewarding Positive Contributions*

Meaningful work is the main motivator, and that should be the starting point for service leaders. You had the opportunity to learn about that in our explanation of Performance Role #9, *Creating Meaning for Everyone*. But beyond this basic intrinsic motivator, the service leader has access to many extrinsic motivators.

The old adage that "people tend to do what they are rewarded for," remains true. What is different in today's fast moving, innovative workplace however, are the behaviors and activities that need to be rewarded. The old contributions such as hard work, getting things done on time, and having a good attitude, etc. are still to be rewarded, but there are some new ones that fit the times.

- Risk taking and winning. Big advances typically require an individual or a team to take risks. Even when good planning precedes a risky innovation, there is the probability of failing. It is good to plan, to win, and to be rewarded. If it all works, people will be even more willing to risk again.

- <u>Risk taking, losing, and learning</u>. Good shot failures, although not much fun, do provide opportunities to learn. Edison learned many, many ways *not* to make a light bulb before he learned how *to* make one. We are told that innovators fail much more often than they succeed. But if so, Total Leaders cut their losses quickly and move on to the next "good shot" idea and plan. When they are successful, they run hard and long with their new market advantage. Service leaders don't reward "shot in the dark" failures, but they do accept and reward "good shot" failures.

- <u>Challenging the status quo</u>. In the stable world of the past, the status quo was why your organization was successful. But in today's world, success is very transitory, and challenging present practices is valued. The service leader must keep from becoming defensive, and instead give off clear signals that challenges and suggestions are not only accepted . . . they're rewarded.

- <u>Committing fully to team efforts</u>. The Lone Ranger, hero in the western days of the past, is not the hero in today's effective organizations. Problems and plans are complex and no one person has the expertise, the time, or the energy to go it alone. The good news here is that learning is social, and it appears to be more fun to win as a team.

If these are the behaviors we want continued, they should be rewarded. But rewarded with what? Rewards too have changed in today's work world . . . maybe they really haven't changed that much and it's just that we have learned more about the power of some of the "soft" rewards. Dollar$, often thought to be the ultimate reward, are not long-term motivators for those who already are having their basic needs met. The service leader's most effective rewards are often soft, personal, and a bit emotional . . .

RECOGNITION: *We want others to know about your success.*

FREEDOM: *You set the agenda . . . we'll get you the resources.*

RESPONSIBILITY: *This is big . . . and we need you and your team to do it.*

ATTABOYS/ATTAGIRLS: *I saw what you did . . . great intervention . . . I appreciate that very much.*

INFLUENCE: *We want you to help us make our big important decisions.*

One small, interesting yet powerful tidbit that we can't help but mention . . . the Gallup people who have done extensive research and writing on what causes people to be engaged in their work have found that answering "yes" to the following question is most predictable of worker engagement. (This might surprise!) *Do you have a best friend at work?*

Chapter 10
Takeaways:

Leadership is key . . . full commitment, full support, and inspirational leadership is required of everyone. Nothing this bold can be accomplished without passion, optimism, and courage.

Consider using Schwahn and Spady's books . . . _Total Leaders 2.0_ and _Learning Communities 2.0_ as your guides . . . everything in this chapter is explained in detail therein.

Education is the most difficult of all industries/professions to change. Be ready for resistance and setbacks, be the keeper of the vision, persevere, and never lose hope . . . change our present Industrial Age schooling to **MCL** and you/we will have changed a large and critical part of our world.

The Evolution of Our Definition of Leadership:

Leadership is influence
to
Leadership is future focused influence
to
Leadership is heartfelt, future focused influence

Chapter 11

The Elementary
MCL Vision

Most elementary teachers are "wired"
for customized learning!

Chuck Schwahn

♪

Chapter 11 Intent

**To clearly show teachers/learning facilitators,
school leaders, and parents
what MASS CUSTOMIZED LEARNING will look like, be like,
and feel like when implemented in an Elementary School.**

Since first publishing *Inevitable* we have frequently been asked how the **MCL** vision might be applied to an elementary school learner and an elementary school teacher. The intent of this new chapter is to describe what an elementary **MCL** school would look and feel like from a teacher's perspective, a school principal's perspective, and a learner's perspective as they begin to implement **MCL**.

Note: This chapter is about the *organizational structure* of a **MCL** elementary school. It is not about curriculum and/or instruction. We will discuss curriculum and instruction only inasmuch as it helps us to be concrete about the structure of a **MCL** school system.

Our vision for a **MCL** elementary school structure differs significantly from the structure of our ideal high school. High schools are structured as one comprehensive and complex organization. When one part of the HS master schedule is changed, it can, and usually does, impact many other aspects of the schedule. The structure of the typical elementary school is not nearly as tightly aligned. One teacher, or a teaching team, can modify their schedule quite freely without impacting any other classrooms.

Therefore, rather than to be very specific about how a **MCL** elementary school should be structured, we will present guidelines that will help teams of teachers create a structure that meets the needs of their specific team and their specific learners. When we created the **MCL** HS vision, we were thinking of 1500 learners and approximately 60 teachers. As we created this **MCL** Elementary School vision, we were thinking of an Elementary School of 400 to 600 learners divided into teams of approximately 75-100 multi-age learners, and 3 or 4 teachers . . . or teams of 3 or 4 "learning facilitators" if you would.

We will be quite firm with "guidelines" that are core to the vision, and a bit less directive with those that we believe are "best" options.

Note: As writers we have made a decision to use words and labels that fit with our perceptions of today's realities; words that we think allow readers to open, update, clarify, and expand their thinking. Our first case in point is that we no longer believe that the label "student" and the label "learner" should be thought of as synonyms. So, in the interest of transparency, let us share our thoughts on the appropriate use of these two labels.

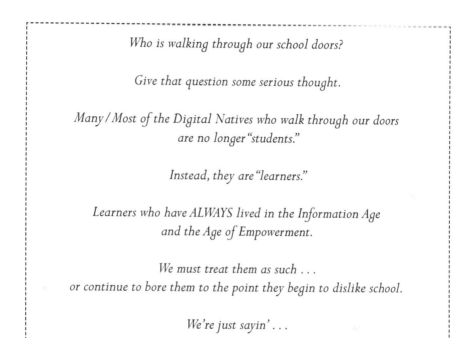

Who is walking through our school doors?

Give that question some serious thought.

Many / Most of the Digital Natives who walk through our doors are no longer "students."

Instead, they are "learners."

Learners who have ALWAYS lived in the Information Age and the Age of Empowerment.

We must treat them as such . . .
or continue to bore them to the point they begin to dislike school.

We're just sayin' . . .

So, for now, please allow us to use the term "learner" when we remember to do so. Words do make a difference as to how we think. When we say or think "Student," it is easy to think . . . Student = container to be filled. When we say or think "Learner," it is easy to think and visualize . . . Learner = teacher as learning facilitator. This is a "not so subtle" shift. Who is responsible for learning when we think of the young boy or girl as a "student?" Now, who is responsible for learning when we think of a young girl or boy as a "learner?" Just to be clear, if one of your school goals is to graduate "lifelong learners," should we educators think of the people walking through our doors as "students" or as "learners."

A MOM'S PERSPECTIVE: HE LOVES LEARNING!

My 8-year-old son, Lincoln, loves school! And, I can see why!

He is challenged every day, learns through content that is interesting to him, and the school has the technology that allows him to go as fast as he can. He really doesn't have much homework because he is so engaged while in school. Still, he chooses to do some of his online learning at home so that he can keep up with or ahead of his buddies. The kid loves learning! I am convinced the MASS CUSTOMIZED LEARNING *approach has much to do with Lincoln's motivation and his achievement.*

Here are some quotes from Lincoln. He and others were interviewed by a local news reporter who did a story on **MCL** *in our schools.*

Lincoln — in his own words:

"School is fun! I have a lot of friends. Skylar is my six-year-old best friend. She's in my Reading Learning Goals seminar. We call them "seminars"— like they do in college. Bradley is my eight-year-old best friend. I work with him on Math Learning Goals using lots of computer games and apps. We can go fast! And Spencer is my ten-year-old best friend. Spencer, me, and other 'scholars' (that's what my teacher calls us) are doing a Community Project seminar for Science and Social Studies. It is about helping stray cats and dogs. I love dogs! And I really like school too!"

How did this happen? How did this elementary school move from an outdated, Industrial Age, assembly-line structure, organized to accommodate administrative conveniences, . . . to an Information Age, Age of Empowerment system with a clear and deep focus on the learning needs of each learner. Well, it happened for two reasons. One, people, . . . everyone, teachers, leaders, parents, and learners clearly recognized the need to improve their school system, and two, the time was right. Mass customizing technology is everywhere in our lives, just waiting to be applied to education and to learning.

Teachers and school leaders are key to educational change in the Elementary School. Until they embrace the need for change and the need for a clear learner-centered focus, not much will, or can, happen to change and improve our outdated structures and practices.

Let's listen to the teachers and school leaders tell the story.....

A TEACHER'S PERSPECTIVE: HER MOTIVATION

(Michelle's Story)

I was teaching second grade at West Elementary when a number of things seemed to fall into place for me and for my teacher friends. Jack McDonough, West Elementary Principal, had given off a number of cues that he wanted to break the old elementary school mold, that he was supportive of change and innovation, and that he was particularly intrigued by the possibilities of team teaching, non-grading, and multi-age grouping.

Jenny, who taught first grade, was on one side of me, and Brooke, who taught third grade, was on the other. We each had more than ten years of experience and, now that I think about it, probably were getting a bit bored with redoing the same thing year after year . . . and also a bit bored with talking in eight-year-old sentences for most of our waking hours! Jenny, Brooke, and I had become good friends — professional friends and personal friends. We enjoyed doing things together outside of school too.

I may have been the one who started talking about the three of us teaming, multi-age grouping, non-grading, and sharing students, but Brooke and Jenny didn't need much convincing. We knew that, in theory anyway, the three of us could meet the needs of 75 learners better than each of us alone could meet the personal learning needs of 25 learners. There was much overlap between the learning needs of first, second, and third grade learners, and we were duplicating the efforts of each other.

We decided to call Jack on his suggestion that we become more innovative and shared our ideas with him. Jack was supportive from the start. He helped us get a common planning time, to have the part-time support of Liz, a very effective teacher aide with values similar to ours, to get the acceptance and support of the rest of the staff, and to talk up our ideas and plans with parents.

We planned off-and-on for the second half of the school year with the intent to start our program at the beginning of the following year. We were quite lucky to have our rooms on the same wing and adjacent to each other. Don't know if the three of us became good friends because our rooms were close together or because we all had similar values and beliefs regarding learning and learners and teachers and teaching. But, bottom line, our project is working well, we feel more professional with what we do, we know that we are better able to meet the learning needs of each child, everyone seems to be satisfied with our results, and we enjoy our work . . . almost every day!

TAKEAWAYS FROM MICHELLE'S STORY

- *The size of the team matters.*

The optimum number of team members is the maximum number of resources the team is able to provide learners while simultaneously keeping the management of the team simple, effective and efficient. Our general rule-of-thumb for primary school teams is three or four. Three is probably best for six- to nine-year olds in a multi-age configuration, while teams of four may be optimum for ten- to twelve-year olds in a multi-age configuration. These numbers are not as rigid as they sound, so think "rule-of-thumb." With each addition of a team member, scheduling becomes more complex and time consuming, but that is not the only reason to control the number of team members. Larger teams are bound to have more personality clashes and relationship problems than will be the norm for smaller teams.

- *Empowered teams are key.*

Teaming becomes a personal thing . . . probably cannot be avoided, nor should it be. There is a psychological reward for team accomplishment and it is said that we humans are "social animals." When we have personally chosen to become part of a team, we tend to do the work to make it work.

But there is a caveat or two here, maybe even a bit of a paradox for the school leader. The staff needs to know that if the vision of the school is based on teaching teams, then teachers have to be able to work in teams. Teacher preferences are important, but schools do not exist for adults, they exist for learners and learning. The school vision cannot be seen as an option. If we are part of that school and, therefore, part of that vision, we have to get on the bus or . . . look for another bus that is going in "my" direction.

Caveat two. It is tempting to put the strongest, most enthusiastic teachers on the same team to give the new vision the best chance of succeeding. That may be a good strategy to get started but, long term, those stars need to be distributed in a way that strengthens all teams. Teaming is a great staff development strategy. Teachers who plan together, work together, and watch each other, learn from each other . . . and they learn the good things. The new "best way" of working with learners becomes the team norm.

- *Changing school structures to improve learning is a "professional" decision.*

Today's Industrial Age schools are structured to be "administratively convenient." Placing learners in single classrooms by dividing the number of learners by the number of teachers and moving them in batches to the next grade each year regardless of their readiness is not about learning . . . it is about administrative convenience. Professionals focus first on the learner, and when there is a better structure for the learner, although maybe more difficult to manage, professionals make the decision to go with the "learner and learning" option.

- *Teaming, non-grading, and multi-age grouping are complementary and synergistic.*

Maybe a note of explanation is necessary here for those who are too young to know Madeline Hunter. "Non-grading" is not about letter grades. It is about ridding ourselves of Grade 1, Grade 2, etc., . . . it is about the assembly-line structure that does not accommodate differing learning rates.

If you are going to do any one of the three, why not do ALL three . . . change is difficult, but bigger changes are not that much more difficult. And the potential payoff is far greater. Our advice and the advice of our advisors — "get in with both feet!"

- *Teams require planning time, effectively structured meetings, and clear records of decisions and expectations.*

189

This statement is true for all teams from all arenas, so expect it also to be true for "team teaching." If no member of the team has the skills to conduct an effective meeting, get some help. And we would suggest that all members work to acquire those skills. Effective teams share leadership responsibilities.

THE LEADER'S PERSPECTIVE: HIS ROLE

(Jack's Story)

I followed a popular principal here at West Elementary. Jim Perry was popular with the students, the staff, and the community . . . and in retrospect, although I am a bit quieter and laid back, Jim and I share many of the same values and ideas about how to improve schools, how to update the old school structures . . . how to bring in a little fresh air if you will.

I have been around for a few years and was highly influenced by Dr. Madeline Hunter, Principal of the UCLA Lab School, when I began my teaching career. Dr. Hunter talked of "Individualized Instruction" and we all knew that it was the right thing to do for learners. But until today's technology came to be, it was difficult if not impossible for one teacher in one classroom to meet the individual needs of 25 learners all at the same time. Some teachers can turn cartwheels with kids and keep all of them motivated all of the time, but they are being successful in spite of our graded, Industrial Age structure, not because of it.

Jim was a bit more flamboyant when sharing his vision for West Elementary than I was, but our visions seemed to be very congruent. He had probably "created the need for change" before I arrived, and my quiet and supportive style probably worked well because of that. Anyway, teachers at West are great — lifelong learners, professionals, have good collegial relationships, and most are eager to try something new if they think it will improve student learning.

In the middle of my first year at West, Michelle and her team came to me with their ideas about teaming. Brooke, Jenny, and Michelle all had good credibility with the staff, with kids, and with parents. It was evident from the beginning that they had given their proposal a good deal of thought . . . their planning and their enthusiasm gave me confidence that they would make it work. I shared my thoughts and ideas with them, but I would say that about 75% of what they have done was their idea.

190

My leadership roles and responsibilities, I believe, are first, to create a vision of what West Elementary will look like when we are operating at our ideal best and meeting the individual learning needs of our learners every hour of every day . . . and to help teachers understand how that vision will impact them personally. When that vision is clear and agreed upon, it then becomes my responsibility to align all resources with that vision.

Let me stop here; I may have made it sound like the West vision was all mine. Not so, the vision belongs to all of us. Everyone has had the opportunity to have input into the West vision . . . but now that that vision is in place, we ALL have the responsibility to get on with it! I believe what Collins said in his <u>Good To Great</u> book: "Leaders get the right people on the bus, the wrong people off of the bus, and the right people in the right seats." Strong, courageous leadership is a <u>requirement</u> if the MASS CUSTOMIZED LEARNING Vision is to become a reality. Flamboyant leaders can be strong and courageous . . . and quiet leaders can be strong and courageous. Style is the variable, strength and courage are the requirements.

Michelle's team is one of our big successes. (By the way, Michelle does not call it "her" team . . . she is very clear that it is OUR team . . . and that is accurate.) They have been and continue to be role models for other teachers and their teaming structure has influenced the structure throughout the school. No two teams in our school are structured exactly alike, but there are some "bottom lines" for us . . . for everyone. In short, before we decide what we will do, we openly and honestly ask and answer the telltale question, "Is this decision about control or about learning?"

TAKEAWAYS FROM JACK'S STORY

- *Strong, supportive leadership is a must.*

   Strong leaders don't expect change to happen by itself; don't expect all good ideas to bubble up from the bottom. They know to involve people in the change process, but they realize that today, leadership, vision, and change are "joined at the hip." That said, when a change has been decided upon, the organizational chart flips and the leader becomes the "service leader,"

191

aligning the organization and its resources to be supportive of those making the changes. Change leaders frequently ask the question, "What can I do . . . or stop doing, that will help you to make your change?"

- *Don't wait for them to come to you.*

Both Jim and Jack gave off cues and vibes that they wanted change to happen at West. Some like Michelle, Jenny, and Brooke took the cues . . . the cues fit their values, beliefs, and desires. Now that's ideal. But it's not enough. Kids are in other classrooms having to wait another year or more until their teacher decides to be part of the change. Strong leaders know that they are learner advocates and ensure that productive change happens . . . sooner rather than later. Learners should not have to wait for someone to retire.

- *Vision provides the motivation for change.*

Leaders are visionaries. Leaders take people to places they would not have gone without them. Leaders must identify or create (with much staff input) a compelling vision, they must communicate that vision with passion, live that vision, and do what they must to get everyone on board.

- *Alignment, the "heavy lifting," makes change happen.*

A truism – behaviors don't change if structures don't change. To change the vision, and not to believe that the structure must change to be aligned with that vision, is naive to say the least. Our present structure is designed perfectly to get the results that we are now getting. If we want different results, we need new and different structures that are tightly aligned with the new vision. Amen.

- *Plan leadership transitions or start from zero.*

Jack, maybe by chance, struck on a big flaw in our leadership selection process when he described his predecessor. He followed Jim, an effective leader whose vision of the ideal West Elementary School was similar to his and who had already started that vision ball rolling. It is rare that district or school leaders are chosen because of their vision. School boards and super-intendents tend to simply look for the best person they can find to replace a departing leader, with little thought given to whether or not the new gal or guy will follow through with the good things that are now happening.

Effective businesses are different. Sure they want a good person to replace the one who is leaving, but they also want one committed to the direction the organization has chosen to take.

- *Getting the right people on the bus.*

Education is a people business. We run because of dedicated teachers and administrators. It follows that personnel must be a central concern for school leaders. We must reward our dedicated, talented, and optimistic people, and we must have the will and courage to remove those who aren't meant for this most important profession.

A LEARNER'S PERSPECTIVE: HIS ENGAGEMENT

Meet Lincoln. Lincoln is an active 8-year-old boy who loves sports of all kinds, is tech savvy like all of his friends (he is, of course, a Digital Native) and, oddly enough, likes to cook . . . checks out cookbooks from the library . . . go figure.

Lincoln's dad is employed by a technology firm and his mom is a part-time employee of a school district. Lincoln has a 10-year-old brother who is a fifth grader and is beginning to dislike school. Brother Thomas attends a traditional graded school known for supportive parents and high test scores. Lincoln also started school in a graded system, but this year was moved to the MASS CUSTOMIZED LEARNING (**MCL**) program. Lincoln looks forward to going to school, does quite well . . . and seldom embarrasses his parents. A pretty good kid!

Lincoln's parents are concerned that electronic gadgets and games might dominate his time, so they limit Lincoln to a maximum of 45 minutes a day on the family computer, his iTouch, and/or his Xbox. Lincoln tends to cheat on this a bit and can usually stretch the 45 minutes to 60. Being a parent today is not easy!

(Lincoln's Comments)

My school is fun because I get to be with my friends and, mostly, we get to do fun things. Last year I was in Mrs. Watson's room . . . she is a first grade teacher. This year my mom and dad signed me up for the teaming room . . . I think that I am a second grader, but I'm not sure. Some kids in my homeroom are older than I am and some are younger . . . so it's hard to tell which grade we are in.

Mrs. Swartz is my homeroom teacher . . . the other teachers call her Brooke . . . but we all do things in all of the classrooms. On Friday when school is getting out, Mrs. Swartz puts up a list of all of us kids on the door, and behind our names she writes the room that we will be in next week to start the day. Sometimes I am in a group that is learning a lesson from my list of learner outcomes and the teacher is telling us what to do, and sometimes, when I am not in any group, I just do my outcomes on a computer or my iPad. I can go as fast as I can when I am doing computer outcomes and sometimes, when my friends are at the same place doing the same thing, we do it together. That's more fun!

Most of my computer lessons are fun but some are kind of boring. I like the ones that are kind of like games . . . where you have to do math or something to get points and win games. Sometimes I do my computer learning at home too, but my mom and dad say that if I work hard in school and get a lot done, I should go outside and play sports with my friends or my brother when I get home from school. But I really want to keep ahead of my friends on my "online" learning outcomes!

On some days we have "specials," that's what Mrs. Swartz calls them . . . some of us go to PE, some to music, and some to the library. We all go at the same time so the teachers don't have anything to do.

I like all of my teachers but Mrs. Swartz is my favorite. I think she likes me. I got to pick her for my homeroom teacher. Some kids didn't get their first pick of homeroom teachers but everyone got their first or second pick.

TAKEWAYS FROM LINCOLN'S COMMENTS

- *Lifelong Learning Starts Here*

Nearly every school system today has a lifelong learning goal for all learners, and they should. But just stating a goal is quite meaningless if the system and its people do not become "intentional" about it. Our favorite Stephen Covey quote is, "If it's important, it should be intentional." Lincoln is being given enough freedom about choices to learn how to make good ones, and enough structure so that he uses his learning time effectively. Just as learners progress at differing rates cognitively, they mature at differing rates regarding the willingness and ability to take responsibility.

- *Grade Levels Disappear*

Learners are grouped according to each one's learning needs rather than artificial "grade levels." Learners are not locked into a "2nd grade" curriculum but are encouraged and supported to advance as fast and far as possible. Learning is personalized to ALL learners, which allows learners to move at their optimum rate and allows the fast runners to run.

- *More Dynamic Learning Environment*

Life outside of school is exciting and dynamic for today's youth. A single teacher and a single classroom don't provide the type of stimulation they are accustomed to. Now there is something to be said about excessive stimulation, but allowing learners to move, experience different settings and different adult personalities has the potential to make the day and learning more exciting.

- *Balancing School and "Being a Kid"*

If the time a learner spends in an elementary school is efficiently and effectively utilized, if the system is designed to create a high ratio of learner time-on-task, there is probably little need for homework . . . or not much homework anyway. There needs to be a balance of learning in interactive groups, for teacher-guided direct instruction, and for online learning. There also needs to be a balance between school work and simply playing and having fun. We sometimes take ourselves and our children a bit too seriously. The key word here is "balance."

TECHNOLOGY: AS A MANAGEMENT SYSTEM

(Michelle's Comments)

Brooke, Jenny, and I actually began teaming, non-grading, and multi-aging about 8 years ago . . . and we did quite well from the start using Madeline Hunter's model and suggestions . . . with our modifications, of course. But two or three years ago, when the new term Mass Customizing moved from an oxymoron to reality, and mass customizing technology became the norm on the Internet, we made a large and significant jump. We moved from teaming and non-grading ala Hunter, to teaming and non-grading ala Apple, Microsoft, YouTube, and Google. Now that statement may need a bit of an explanation! Let me use an "Apple and music" example and comparison.

Remember when we had to buy a CD to be able to get the one or two songs that we really liked? Well, Apple changed all of that, you might say "mass customized" all of that, with the iPod and iTunes. Apple made it possible to purchase for 99 cents nearly any song that has ever been sung. I can download Abba's "Take a Chance on Me" and be listening to it on my computer or iPod in less than a minute. Apple later realized that they could also download movies, TV shows, and just about anything else using their iTunes system. *Then they started the online Apple Store selling everything they market and added the store to their very successful iTunes* management and delivery system. *Now, "iTunes" doesn't even sound like the label that Apple should use for what has become their management system. Two years ago, a similar turn of events happened in our* MASS CUSTOMIZED LEARNING *project. Note that we no longer call our system teaming and non-grading but have given it the up-to-date label of* MASS CUSTOMIZED LEARNING . . . *or* **MCL** *for short.*

So . . . for the comparison to Apple. Our project started to change significantly when we stopped giving letter grades and replaced them with electronic learner portfolios for each learner . . . we now call them "ePortfolios." In the beginning we just thought that it would be good to document the learning of each child. We could then show learners and their parents exactly what the children had done to prove that they had mastered a learner outcome. In many cases the documentation takes the form of a written or typed document, like a test or a written statement. But with the popularity of YouTube and Facebook, we realized that audio or video recordings would fit nicely into a learning portfolio . . . and add a little pizzazz for the learner and the parent. Parents loved it and the ePortfolio added a lot to our **MCL** project. But, like with Apple and downloading songs . . . that was just the beginning.

We rather quickly realized that the ePortfolio was also a great way of staying in communication with parents. Parents can now access their child's ePortfolio online at any time 24/7. We quickly learned that we could also coach parents on how they could support their child in the specific learner outcome their child was working through at present. But then, voila, Jenny insightfully put two-and-two together and realized that we could use ePortfolios to quickly and effectively group students for learning. With one or two clicks we are now able to identify which of our 75 learners are in need of working on any specific learner outcome . . . and, equally importantly, identify those who also have mastered the prerequisite learnings required to successfully master this new learner outcome. Where we used to have to go through 75 written documents to group learners, we can now identify those with similar needs with a couple of clicks.

Sounds easy, but it took a lot of work to create the programs to do all of this, and a lot of time to input the records of each learner. Now that it's all up and running, we are more able to ensure that we are meeting the learning needs of each learner each hour of every day. So, just as iTunes has become Apple's management system, ePortfolios have become the management system of our **MCL** program.

THE SCHOOL SYSTEM'S "TO DO" LIST

(Jack's Comments)

*Michelle made all of that sound rather natural and easy, and although all of our efforts and spent resources were worth it, let me list what my office and the District Office needed to do to make today's **MCL** vision a reality. We needed to be cost conscious of course, and the work was significant. The payoff for our efforts and costs came with the success of this first **MCL** team. We have continued to improve the ePortfolio technology and ePortfolios are now our "grading system" and "report cards"... and much of our management system throughout the elementary schools in our district.*

☑ Vision Building

In today's rapidly changing world, it is critical that leaders be visionaries, that the organization have a rather concrete picture of where it is headed, and that everyone in the organization knows how that vision will impact them. For visions to be powerful, they must run well ahead of the organization's present capacity to make them happen. Visions do not "push" people into a change. Rather, visions "pull" people into the change . . . "we want that so bad that we will work to make it happen." As principal, it was my responsibility and that of the District Office . . . with heavy and heated input from the faculty . . . to create and sell the **MCL** vision to the West Elementary staff.

☑ Curriculum as Outcomes

This one is big, big as in "important" . . . and also a very large task. To do it right, the process of identifying learner outcomes should begin with an in-depth, future-focused, learner-centered strategic design process. The Superintendent and the Board of Education have the responsibility to create this strategic design. But if they have not done so, we can't stop the process of vision building at the school level and getting on with the creation of **MCL** opportunities for our present learners. State learning standards may be the best place to look for credible learner outcomes if the local district has not systematically created its own. Bottom line: for **MCL** to work, teachers . . . and everyone else . . . must know what we want our learners to know, be able to do, and "be like" when they complete our programs and walk out our doors. Without clear learner outcomes, everything else a school system does is a shot in the dark.

☑ ePortfolio Technology

The technology to systematically create electronic learning portfolios exists today. Many people seeking jobs today have created exciting electronic portfolios that communicate their talents and accomplishments. Our computers have hard drive space to store portfolios, our cameras, smartphones, and iPads make the creation of videos routine, and YouTube shows us how they can be stored and accessed. But that is not to say that it was a snap to put those technologies together to create a system with the capacity that makes the documentation, storage, and accessibility of learner outcome mastery routine. Bottom line is that it can be done and we have to do it to have an effective and efficient **MCL** management system.

☑ Staff Development

When Michelle and her team moved from self-contained classrooms to teaming, and later when they embraced technology as a management system, they didn't forget what they knew about good teaching. Going to **MCL** does not mean that you "throw the baby out with the bathwater." That said, **MCL**, coupled with our strong belief that we need to create lifelong learners, requires the role of the teacher to morph from "teacher as teller" into "teacher as learning facilitator." And teaming *does* change many of the dynamics of teaching. The Lone Ranger is dead and "the team" is the new entity. Positive and supportive professional relationships become requirements. Staff development comes easier when your school has one or more effective teams already in place. Teachers and teams new to the experience can observe, work with existing teams, and share ideas and concerns with those who have worked through the struggles. Staff development needs, when moving to **MCL**, are rather easy to identify and not that difficult to manage . . . but everyone needs to feel confident that they can make the switch if we are going to have "happy campers."

☑ **Community Understanding and Acceptance**

Our community trusts our teachers. . . and should. We have a great staff, good people who believe in kids and make their classrooms safe and inviting places for young, eager learners. Michelle and her team met with the parents of their learners on several occasions prior to making the switch to **MCL**. I, of course, met with the parents too, and was emphatic about the choice that each of them had to opt out of this first attempt to implement the **MCL** vision. No one requested that his or her child be removed from the program. Eventually, **MCL** and teaming were implemented throughout our school. It was not considered a "pilot," or a "special project." It became the norm of how we deliver learning for all learners. (An aside here . . . I believe very strongly that if the idea is a good one, that it makes sense, that it is logical, that it holds great potential, that it is being proposed by trustworthy people . . . most people will embrace it and thank you for making the change happen. AND, **MCL** makes a lot more sense to anyone who has children than does our present time-based assembly line, which everyone knows is inconsistent with how kids learn. Excuse me for that mini-rant . . . couldn't help myself!)

TECHNOLOGY: AS TEACHER

(Michelle's Comments)

Our kids today are all . . . or nearly all . . . tech savvy. They are Digital Natives, and we adults are the Digital Immigrants. They come to us as successful and confirmed learners. Watch their faces and note the confidence when they pick up a smartphone, a Game Boy, or an iPad. Manuals that used to come with the new technology toys are obsolete. When eight-year-olds encounter a new technology, they just "start." They are naturally intuitive (you see, they ARE Digital Natives) and they seem to have a direct Wi-Fi connection with the person who created the program. No fear; you can always start over; failure is a learning tool; they have never heard of "whiteout." (By the way, if you remember "whiteout," you are definitely a Digital Immigrant!)

When online learning came on the scene in earnest a few years ago, our team, in their spare time, started surfing the Internet to check out the availability of online learning for the type of learner outcomes that are part of our curriculum. We found some early, we were intrigued, they kept coming, we got interested, and when Apple and the applications (apps) arrived we were hooked. We learned that many of the learner outcomes that we wanted our learners to master . . . especially those foundational learner outcomes . . . are available somewhere online. We also had to admit that although much of online instruction is poorly designed and clumsy, some of the online instruction taught some of our learner outcomes better . . . and with more patience . . . than we did.

We got excited about the possibility of using computers and iPads to teach a portion of our outcomes . . . but which learner outcomes? Brooke stepped in with a critical insight. She suggested that we go through our learner outcomes one-by-one, and then ask the professional question, "How is this learner outcome best learned?" Note that Brooke didn't suggest that we ask, "How is this learner outcome best taught?" Professionals are client-centered; professional educators are learner-centered. Many outcomes at our learner level are best learned through direct instruction and guided practice, many are best learned through individual and group projects, many are learned through group discussion . . . but many could also be learned best using the customizing technology of the day. Apple and Android apps are great examples of what is now available . . . and new educational apps are arriving daily.

After answering the "professional question" about each of our learner outcomes, we calculated that approximately 50% or ½ of all learner outcomes could be effectively and efficiently learned with/by "technology as teacher." Now, that new reality might scare some teachers who fear that they are going to be replaced by computers. But that will never happen. _The most critical learner outcomes are deep and complex._ These learner outcomes having to do with life skills, thinking skills, attitudes, values, etc., require the skills and guidance of a professional educator, a professional learning facilitator.

> *Oh, but the glass is half full, SHOUTS Michelle, the optimist! If 50% of our learner outcomes can be learned best through technology, didn't our student/teacher ratio just get cut in half? Don't we now have something of high worth for ½ of our learners to be doing while we are working with a smaller group of learners who needs ME for this learner outcome? When can we start!*

THE SCHOOL SYSTEM'S "TO DO" LIST

(Jack's Comments)

The "Technology as Teacher," as Michelle and her team labeled it, required a whole lot of work for our District Office, particularly from the Curriculum and Instruction Department. And that's as it should be. If our district was to leave the Industrial Age and move to "the Age of Empowerment" driven by Information Age technology, the curriculum and instruction people should be leading the charge. But this was all new for them too, and it took a good deal of cooperation and give-and-take between the District Office and the West staff . . . me included.

*It took a while for the curriculum people to understand West's **MCL** vision, but once they did, they realized the potential **MCL** had for transforming our approach to meeting the learning needs of every learner every day. They also quickly realized that the West **MCL** vision, if successful, would quickly spread throughout our system. By the way, our Superintendent, Allison, was most helpful with her support. She made sure that the leadership team understood our **MCL** vision and its implications for everyone in the system, and made an "update on our project" a regular item on our leadership team meeting agenda. Allison was a support, an advocate and, really, quite a cheerleader for us. She kept the Board informed, spoke about our project at service club meetings, and would do her "90-second elevator speech to anyone who would listen."*

The Curriculum and Instruction Department, quite naturally, was the district focal point for helping our team to identify and clearly describe the expected learner outcomes for our elementary school learners. Julie, our Assistant Superintendent for Curriculum and Instruction, committed her department to identify and clearly articulate learner outcomes for our total system . . . we now know what we want all learners to know, be able to do, and be like when they graduate from our system. These learner outcomes of course include our state standards, most of which are already defined in a learner outcome format.

But being capable of making a significant portion of the system's learner outcomes available online only begins with identification and articulation of the learner outcomes. Let me list what must happen at the district level if this critical component of the **MCL** *vision, "online learning made available 24/7," is to be "ready for rollout."*

☑ **Identification of Learner Outcomes Best Learned Online**

I talked with you about this before, but it is so important that I will review it again. For anyone to be held accountable for learners learning, we must first identify what it is that we want our learners to know, be able to do, and to be like . . . "be likes" includes attitude, values, personal skills, work ethic, etc. (A side note: . . . It's interesting to know that Daniel Goleman, the recognized expert regarding this topic, states that one's "emotional quotient" or "be like" is twice as important as one's "intelligence quotient" when predicting lifelong success and happiness. So, the "be like" part of learner outcomes is not something just warm and fuzzy.) Now back to "learner outcomes best learned online" . . . we obviously must have made those decisions before we began the steps necessary to put those learner outcomes "online." A hint about selecting those outcomes best learned online – the more learner outcomes that we can put in that category, with integrity of course, the more time teachers . . . excuse me, the more time "learning facilitators" will have to teach learners those important outcomes that require a skilled professional.

☑ Finding Where Online Learning Opportunities Are Available Online

Learning opportunities for nearly any learner outcome that we can think of are online somewhere. Some are good, some are very good, some not so good, and some really bad. Just getting teachers to start looking for learner outcomes for the developmental level of their learners is an exercise that helps teachers become comfortable with online learning. Looking for Apple or Android apps that teach basic skills and concepts is a good start for beginners. Apps may one day rule the world of online learning. Unless something comes along to make "apps" obsolete of course.

☑ Getting Permission to Access Our Online Learning Choices

Many of the best online learning opportunities are free or available for a small charge. Some are a bit pricey but worth the dollars. When teachers find online learning opportunities that they want to make available for their learners, we ask them to contact the Curriculum and Instruction Office so that they can check them out as to effectiveness, price, and legality. We don't want to get into any legal hassles that may impact our **MCL** program.

☑ Creating the Programs for Learners to Access the Online Learning Activities

Identifying effective online learning opportunities may be the easiest part of the online learning process. Creating the programs that make it easy and quick for learners to access online learning opportunities is not so easy. We are a work in progress here, still a bit slow and clunky. Our IT people are on board and improving our system nearly every day . . . and we expect that, given the movement toward **MCL**, sophisticated and smooth commercial programs will be available in the near future that make online learning opportunities easy to access.

☑ Creating and Integrating the ePortfolio System

The electronic portfolio system is the key to managing a **MCL** program. Not only is it at the heart of the individual learner's needs, but it is the backbone of our system for grouping learners, for creating accountability systems, and for determining the overall success of our **MCL** program. The technology to accomplish this aspect of our instructional delivery system is being used extensively today. We just need to apply those technologies to our **MCL** program. And it's coming. It IS Inevitable.

LEARNING OPPORTUNITIES: GROUPING & REGROUPING LEARNERS EFFECTIVELY

There are nearly as many ways of grouping children for learning opportunities as there are teaching teams. No two teams do it exactly the same, but there are some underlying rules, guidelines, or "musts" that characterize "professional" teams. Grouping and regrouping learners effectively requires that:

- Teachers are clear regarding learner outcomes. In the end, what must the learner be able to do to demonstrate that he/she has mastered the intended learning outcome?

- There are accurate and easily accessible records of the learner outcomes that each child has mastered, and those outcomes that he/she has not mastered. (It is most helpful to teachers if these records are in the form of electronic learner portfolios.)

- Grouping is based on the learner's cognitive learning needs, but also on his/her social and emotional needs.

- Grouping is flexible, allowing learners to be moved from one group to another when an original diagnosis appears to be inappropriate.

- Grouping must NOT be, or become, based upon the perceived "ability" of each learner. **MCL** grouping is flexible and based upon the learner's here-and-now learning needs . . . and should not be confused with "ability grouping."

(Michelle's Comments about Grouping and Regrouping Learners)

When visitors come to our school to see our **MCL** team in operation, they always ask us how we group our kids, why are these learners in this particular group, how do the children know where to go, do these groups change or are they like the "blackbirds, redbirds, and bluebirds." In a way, the process we use for grouping is very complex . . . a computer program couldn't even do it. But in another way, a more practical way, the grouping process our team uses is quite simple.

To begin with, our team is experienced and each of us has a good understanding of the learner outcomes that are typically important for learners in this age span. We also know that age is not a very good indicator of what a learner needs right now. Some learners, even at this young age (6-9), are one or two years ahead of the norm and some are one or two years behind that norm. And what we are referring to when we say "ahead of" or "behind" makes a big difference. We have learners who read way ahead of expectations but don't know how to relate to other kids. So "ahead of" or "behind" is learner outcome specific. It's very important for a teacher to understand that there are many ways of being smart, of being intelligent, of being "ahead" or "behind." By the way, our team is quite clear about our beliefs regarding learners and learning! Our flexible grouping strategies are driven by those beliefs.

Let me talk you through the process we used this past week to group our learners for what you would have seen happening in our classrooms today. We are not telling anyone that this is the way that they should do it, but this is the way we do it . . . and it is working for us and for our learners. If it didn't work, we would change it . . . and that has happened a time or two in the past.

We tend to regroup our learners every week or two, depending upon how much time we think we need for learners to accomplish the current learner outcomes. Remember now, about 40% to 50% of our learners, at any time, are probably working through the learner outcomes that are best learned through online learning. This allows for groups that might be receiving direct instruction to be significantly smaller, which in turn allows teachers to provide more personalized help. MASS CUSTOMIZED LEARNING *could not happen in the learner's primary years if it were not for teachers who can "customize learning" for kids while they are part of a group. We get good at that! Yah, the computer has helped us a lot with our* **MCL** *project, but we give those computers a head start by being skilled at looking Susie in the eye, smiling, and showing her how to do something . . . while not missing a beat with the rest of the group.*

But let me be more specific. Last Thursday, when we were planning for the week that began this Monday, we began by celebrating the successes of our groups over the past seven days. We do it a bit differently each time we do our planning, but for this meeting we celebrated by telling stories about two or three kids who exceeded our expectations big time. We also talked about a few who struggled and may need a push or hug in the next few days.

Our next step was to review and study the district's learner outcomes. What are the learner outcomes for this age span, which outcomes have our learners mastered, which outcomes follow the sequence of those mastered, which outcomes might be linked with, or be complementary to, other learner outcomes . . . and through this process, discussion, and debate reach consensus as to which learner outcomes to tackle next.

We like to look for a mix of learner outcomes . . . some affective and some cognitive or skill based . . . so that we can mix up our groupings. Of course there are exceptions, but we typically group learners according to their present level of outcome achievement when working on cognitive or skill-based outcomes, and group learners quite randomly, mixing ages, when working on affective learner outcomes. For example, when grouping for reading skills, we work to get learners into the group that best fits their particular reading level. Some children learn faster than others so the groups are constantly changing. When grouping for the more affective learner outcomes, those having to do with attitude, motivation, values, and behavior, we prefer cross-age peer grouping where the more mature can act as coaches of the younger children . . . and both can learn life-role skills in the process. The younger learns what to do and how to do it, and the more mature kid learns how to coach and support and, in the process, experiences the joy of helping others . . . who knows, maybe his / her first experience creates the path to becoming a teacher — the world's most important profession!

TEAM PLANNING

(Michelle's Comments)

Now this is going to sound a bit more formal than it really is, but to help those who are going to implement **MCL** *in an elementary school, I will divide our planning activities into three parts.*

SHORT/QUICK MEETINGS

We meet every morning for about 5 minutes, coffee mugs in hand, (about 30 minutes before our learners arrive) to share ideas or concerns about what the day might hold for us. We meet again for a short time . . . usually 5-10 minutes after we see that last cute little guy, baseball glove in hand, run up the steps and disappear into the school bus . . . to share our brief assessment of the day. If the events of the day require more time, we of course take the time necessary to ensure that things keep running smoothly. We have just started using a private Wiki/blog to communicate among the team. So, we can do so in our own timeframe. We are still a bit clunky at this . . . the Digital Immigrants that we are . . . but know we will get better at it.

MEETINGS TO GROUP LEARNERS

These are important meetings; these are meetings with a solid focus on the needs of our learners. We typically regroup students every 5 to 10 school days, based upon learner needs. We go into a new grouping with a particular number of days in mind to aid in our planning, but we stay flexible about endings. Our purpose for grouping and regrouping learners is based upon the need for learners to demonstrate those general learner outcomes that are best learned through direct instruction, learner/teacher or learner/learner interaction, or individual or group projects. We do our very best to place students into groups that meet their individual learning level, take advantage of one of their best learning modes, and allow them to learn with content of high interest.

Our ePortfolio system is a very big help when it comes to grouping learners for instruction. With a couple of quick clicks we can identify those learners who need a specific learner outcome and who also have the prerequisite learnings that help to ensure a successful learning experience.

After 8-plus years of experience, we are all quite good at identifying the content that will be of high interest for our learners. It sounds complex, but we know our learners well, and typically within an hour or so, are able to decide which learner outcomes will best serve our learners, how those learner outcomes can be best learned, which of us will take responsibility for which set of learner outcomes, and which learners will be in which group. We usually do this planning a few days in advance of the new groupings so that we have time to gather materials and be ready for that exciting first day for everybody . . . kids and teachers.

Our "grouping" meetings are quite organized. We have an agenda, come having thought through a few possibilities, remind ourselves to stay learner focused, do our best to stay on task, make our decisions regarding groups and grouping, and stay flexible enough in our plans that we can move kids from one group to another anytime we think that is in the learner's best interests.

ANNUAL PLANNING MEETINGS

At least once a year we meet with Principal McDonough to talk about how things are going, changes that we might want to make, and to make suggestions as to what he might do to support our work, our team. These meetings usually take place sometime during the summer, after we have had time to reflect on the successes and concerns of the past year, but early enough to do some good thinking before the bells start ringing again.

We also meet with Principal McDonough any time there is a concern or an opportunity that warrants all of us being together to make a decision, but we have this Annual Meeting blocked out to ensure that there is an opportunity for an in-depth review of our processes and achievements at a minimum of once a year. In today's rapidly changing world, what we did this year is not good enough for next year.

It's great to have an effective, optimistic leader who trusts and honors our professionalism. Jack is a great support and is always open to playing the role of "servant leader" once we have agreed on a meaningful purpose and mission. Sometime during our annual sessions you can expect him to slowly and emphatically ask us, "What can I do, or stop doing, that will help you to accomplish your **MCL** vision,". . . and then he actually listens! We also know that Jack will not hesitate to let us know what he thinks and to suggest changes that he thinks are in the best interest of learners.

Learning and supporting has been a two-way street for Jack and our team. We get Jack's encouragement and support and Jack learns things about our operation that he has been able to share with other teams that are forming throughout our school.

CONTINUOUS IMPROVEMENT OF MEETINGS

Jenny, Brooke, and I are close professional colleagues and we are also rather close personal friends who spend time together outside of our work. This is both good news and "cautionary" news. It would be easy to allow our meetings to be a meshing of personal and professional topics and issues . . . and we don't have time for that during our busy work schedule.

So, we intentionally structured our "grouping student" meetings to ensure that we stay on task. We have a set agenda, we take turns facilitating meetings and being the recorder, and we take the time to "process" our meetings while the content, the exchanges, and the decisions are fresh in our minds. We want to know what we did that made the meeting effective, what we might have done that got us off track, what changes we will make for our next meeting, and "do we still like each other." Our meetings have become more effective and efficient over the years that we have worked together . . . and we still like each other.

GETTING STARTED

(Bea)

Our readers will want something concrete about how they might actually plan, organize, and implement a five- or ten-day plan for their learners. Can you give us something that would help a team of teachers understand the process . . . like a step 1, step 2, step 3 kind of thing?

(Michelle's Response)

OK, let me try. But know upfront that no two situations will be exactly alike. I won't go into minute details or this will get too lengthy, but I will attempt to explain the process to the point that an experienced teacher / learning facilitator will be able to fill in the blanks.

Let's say that we have three learning facilitators with approximately 75 multi-age learners who would make up grades 1 through 3 in a traditional school . . . and now they want to team, non-grade, and multi-age. Let's further assume that the school system . . . better called the learning community . . . has clearly identified learner outcomes for their entire system and that those outcomes best learned online are indeed available to learners online. I am also going to assume that this system has created an ePortfolio system as described earlier in your book.

*These assumptions may be far beyond those school systems just beginning to dream and create a **MCL** vision, but I will start this step-by-step process based on these assumptions so that your readers can get right into the organizational structure part of "**MCL** for the Elementary School."*

Bea and Chuck's Note: Not having the aforementioned assumptions in place shouldn't deter a team from going for a **MCL** vision just because everything needed for it to work is not yet in place. Michelle and her team started their **MCL** program with none of these prerequisites in place and were quite successful before they had a topnotch online system or ePortfolios.

(Michelle Continues)

A quick aside here — our team is made up of three women. It would be good, more ideal, if there were a man on our team. We have boys in our school who could sure use a positive male role model in their lives.

Step 1

Study the ePortfolios of your 75 learners. In the old days, this was a very subjective task, but today we can easily aggregate learner portfolios and find where children quite naturally group themselves. Expect upfront that, with three learning facilitators, you will be able to do approximately nine different groups throughout a typical day. I say nine, because each teacher should be able to work with three groups throughout the day, there are three learning facilitators . . . which makes it possible to provide nine learning options each day.

Study the aggregate group learner profile and select eight to ten learner outcomes that accommodate the learning needs of the most learners. We find that we are typically able to group two or three learner outcomes that are closely related into one chunk, which allows us to be more efficient and effective with our time . . . and makes it more exciting for the kids. When you have done this, the next question has to be . . . "Does this grouping allow us to meet meaningful learner outcomes for all of our learners?" This question, of course, will require some subjective but professional decisions to be made . . . keeping learners and learning as the focus. Nothing this complex can be perfect for everyone every hour of every day, but we work to get as close as we can.

Step 2

Let's talk a bit about organizational structure here. Although all schools are different, I think we can assume that we will have time for two learning groups in the morning and one learning group in the afternoon. I'm thinking about timeframes for each group of about an hour and 15 minutes, which would leave time for passing, recess, the special classes like music and P.E., and anything else that needs to be done. This is about grouping and about time . . . as they say, "You do the math!" "You" being the teaching / learning team, of course.

Set up a flexible block schedule if you would like, one similar to the way many middle schools are organized. BUT, keep it flexible. Don't let the schedule get ahead of learner needs or you will only have created another assembly line.

Step 3

Identify which teacher / learning facilitator will be responsible for each outcome or chunk of learner outcomes. This is a time to mix it up . . . if you were the first grade teacher before non-grading, don't slip into the habit of always accepting assignments for the younger children . . . we want non-grading, we want it to look like non-grading, to feel like non-grading. But do select something that you know you are good at teaching, that you have good ideas about what you will do, and something that won't require you to do a great deal of prep to be ready.

A caution is necessary here. We need to remember that we are grouping for **learner outcomes.** *We are not grouping for general levels of achievement or for "intelligence." If we don't want to fall into the trap of achievement grouping, we must take care to ensure that grouping is <u>flexible and that it changes frequently</u>.*

Step 4

Identify the group of learners who will join each learning group . . . this decision, of course, is based upon individual learner needs. We find it best to do the skills-type outcomes in the morning and the more general and subjective outcomes that have to do with relationships, communication, etc. in the afternoon. Age, to some degree, is an indicator of the skills learners need to master, and so our skills groupings are not quite as mixed as to age as are our more general outcomes. We find it exciting to see what happens when learners of significantly different ages work together. It provides an opportunity for us to help children acquire the "soft" but critical skills of communication, relationship building, teaching, leading, problem solving, creating, etc. You can probably tell that these learning opportunities excite me!

Step 5

Build in the online learning time from the beginning. Online learning provides the flexibility that helps to ensure that every learner, every hour, of every day is learning something that is part of his/her learning plan. So, not all learners need to be part of a learning group at the same time . . . in fact, they should not be if the team is utilizing its technology efficiently and effectively. Those learners who did not fit into one or more of the three groups of the day are excellent candidates for online learning. This allows the learning groups to be smaller and provides learning facilitators with opportunities to work one-on-one while also leading a group.

Our team set an expectation that most learners will be working online about one-third of their time. It varies, of course, and we are not afraid to let learners go up to 50% or 60% if online learning is their thing and they are advancing. Technology allows us to meet the needs of all kids . . . those needing more time to master a skill get more time, and the fast runners are allowed to run. We truly meet the learning needs of all learners . . . at both ends of the continuum.

(A Michelle Hint) We have a teacher aide part time . . . wish that she were full time . . . who manages and supervises our online learning. She is very good, knows more about technology than we do, and also knows kids. Mrs. Junek is "connected" in this community and she has formed a "parent volunteer" group to help her / us with the management of online learning. Our volunteers love it. They know that they are given something meaningful to do and they are a great support for our **MCL** *program in the community. There is no horsing around in our online learning centers and our online learning opportunities are getting better all the time. The children especially like those programs that are designed around games and those that provide a reward for mastering a skill . . . a miniclip game is a big motivator for many primary school learners.*

Step 6

Create a simple system for getting learners to where they need to be for their learning opportunity. We regroup learners on average every five to ten learning days. When we regroup (usually at the end of a week) we let them know where they will be going on Monday and we place listings on each door. Brooke, Jenny, and I mostly stay in our rooms and the children move from room to room. They like the movement and we like the security of our desk and our stuff. Today's technology does not require a large backpack. We look forward to the day when each learner has an iPad9 or an Amazon Fire, and it's not that far away. This week the Fire is selling for $199 and textbook costs have gone out of sight. Just thought, when all have an electronic tablet, learners will have their own homepage that includes their schedule . . . as well as their ePortfolio, their assignments, their online learning opportunities, notifications to their parents, their horoscope . . .

Hey Chuck and Bea . . . any questions?

(Chuck)

No, I think that kinda takes care of it for me, Michelle. (Bea leans over and whispers to Chuck, "WOW! We need to clone her!! The ultimate learning facilitator!")

Chapter 11
Takeaways:

The MASS CUSTOMIZED LEARNING vision fits very well in the elementary school.

The **MCL** vision is best implemented by teaching teams, working with multi-age learners, in a non-graded system.

Most elementary teachers/learning facilitators are "wired" for customized learning.

A special "thank you" for some people who helped us to build this Elementary MCL Vision:

Karen Caprio, Director of Curriculum, RSU 15, Gray, ME

Christine Chamberlain, Director of Curriculum, RSU 2, Hallowell, ME

Jeanne Cowan, Technology and Innovation In Education, Rapid City, SD

Janet Hensley, Technology and Innovation In Education, Rapid City, SD

Linda Laughlin, Assistant Superintendent, RSU 18, Oakland, ME

Lori Lodge, Director of Curriculum, RSU 57, Waterboro, ME

Denise Plante, Assistant Superintendent, Jackman, ME

Tom Rooney, Assistant Superintendent, Lindsay School District, Lindsay, CA

Chapter 12

WIIFYs

"The Schooling Dilemma:
Standardized Testing versus Customized Learning"

Clayton Christenson

"If I'd asked my customers what they wanted,
they'd have said a faster horse."

Henry Ford

Our feedback from early readers has made it clear that what we are asking for is massive, systemic, transformational change . . . and that change of this scope, in a very mature industry or profession, is most difficult to initiate, to implement, and to sustain. We agree. We had to. The feedback left us no choice. Welcome to authentic and courageous leadership.

The good news is that although making MASS CUSTOMIZED LEARNING the new mode of operation is difficult, we are also more convinced than ever that the **MCL** vision is very desirable, is doable with courageous, passionate, and tenacious leadership, is worth it to the learner, the parent, the educator, and our society, and we have no choice . . . **MCL** is indeed *Inevitable.* It will happen. When will it be done, who will do it, and how will it be done are questions waiting to be answered. We hope that it will happen sooner than later, that the change will be led by professional educators (like you!), and that it will be done with the learner's wellbeing at the heart of all decisions.

WIIFYs

What's In It For You? What are your WIIFYs? To leave you highly motivated to embrace **MCL** and the change process, we leave you with some solid reasons/rationale to "go for it."

WIIFYs for LEARNERS

* Having your personal learning needs met every hour of every day.
* The opportunity to learn at your optimum rate of speed . . . to advance as far as time and motivation allow.
* The elimination of fear of failure and boredom when you are able to determine what and how you learn.
* Learning opportunities in a number of formats . . . moving from learning based on lectures and listening to learning with interaction, involvement, and relevance.
* Technology-based learning that closely matches the natural learning activities available in gaming activities and social networks.
* The opportunity for "real world" learning from people (coaches/mentors) who are doing it for real.
* The opportunity to observe successful adults collaborating, supporting, and teaming to solve problems and reach goals.

WIIFYs for TEACHERS

* The opportunity to coach and mentor individual learners over a period of time.
* Teaching a skill, concept or process for which all learners have the prerequisite learnings.
* An organizational structure that allows you to apply powerful intrinsic learner motivators.
* Moving the ratio of work from management to professional activities.
* Individualizing instruction . . . something you have always wanted to do.
* Teaming with the NetGeners to continually master the new technologies.
* Entering into a shared rather than near total responsibility for learner achievement.
* Fewer discipline problems as we move from extrinsic to intrinsic learner motivators.
* The opportunity to work/team with other professionals across disciplines toward shared goals . . . and to grow professionally in the process.
* Networking with teachers (local, national, and international) to collaborate in the creation of new systems and strategies in "cutting edge" school systems.
* Learning how other disciplines mesh with yours when helping learners demonstrate life-role learner outcomes.
* The positive feelings that accompany thinking and acting as a true professional.

WIIFYs for LEADERS

* The opportunity to move from the role of school manager to that of a transformational leader.
* The opportunity to be future focused, innovative, courageous, excited, and passionate about what you do.

---

* Moving learners from extrinsic motivators and "compliance" to intrinsic motivators and "empowerment," and thereby eliminating most student discipline concerns.
* The peace of mind that comes with knowing you are doing the right thing . . . that decisions are not made for administrative convenience but are based on what is best for learners.
* The opportunity to make your chosen work lead to a most purposeful life.
* Students regularly learning in the community will help community members to understand and, consequently, to be supportive of the school system.
* The opportunity to feel the pride and receive the recognition that goes with leading an innovative, progressive, learner-centered organization.

WIIFYs for PARENTS

* Children who graduate empowered for their future . . . be that college, work, or another choice.
* Children who are motivated to learn and able to learn at a rate independent of other learners.
* Children who have fewer complaints about school.
* The opportunity to closely monitor the day-to-day activities of your children, to monitor their achievements, and to directly support their learning.

WIIFYs for OUR PROFESSION

* Educators empowered to apply our best research regarding learners and learning.
* Organizational flexibility that allows the profession to quickly incorporate future trends and evolving research.
* The ability to attract the best and brightest to enter this most important profession . . . and the meaningful work will foster educational careers.

---

* The pride that goes with being and acting as a true professional.
* Having learners working more directly with the community obligates the community to have "skin in the game."

WIIFYs for OUR ECONOMY

* Self-directed, lifelong learners who are empowered to contribute to organizations competing in a global economy.
* Learners/graduates who have advanced to the maximum of their ability and are ready to contribute to the continuous improvement of organizations.
* Empowered graduates who are not fearful of trying out their entrepreneurial ideas.

WIIFYs for OUR SOCIETY

* Graduates who are self-directed, lifelong learners who have been thoughtfully and intentionally prepared to be contributing members of society.
* Graduates who have been purposefully and intentionally prepared for success in the critical spheres of living.
* Learners learning in the community will allow students to act as ambassadors for the school system.

We could go on and on about the **MCL** WIIFYs, but we will stop with some of the major reasons and motivations for embracing the **MCL** vision.

Moral Obligation

Larry Lezotte, a leading authority regarding effective schools and school reform, was kind enough to review and react to parts of *Inevitable*. Dr. Lezotte suggested that we educators not only have a professional obligation to make our schools all they can be, but that we also have a moral obligation to do so. Good point, Larry! We agree! Totally! Educators . . . your humble authors surely included . . . are blessed to be doing such purposeful, meaningful, and enjoyable work. We are part of the world's most important profession. With that comes some serious responsibilities and obligations.

In short, we educators have a moral obligation to become the best we can be as we impact the lives of young learners. Beyond that, we educators have a moral responsibility to make our school system the best *it* can be. That moral obligation requires each of us to be a student of the future, to be open to new ideas, to be visionaries continually asking ourselves "what if," and to willingly and courageously risk one's self in organizational efforts to create significant and meaningful learner-centered change. Acting on that moral obligation for meaningful change is surely required when attempting a change as systemic and powerful as MASS CUSTOMIZED LEARNING (Just thought . . . is guilt a motivator? Will ask Larry the next time we see him.)

Appendix: Epilogue:

But Wait, There's More!

*"Courage is
the art of being the only one
who knows you're scared to death."*

British Prime Minister Harold Wilson

*"In the end, you are your best resource.
Go for it!"*

Chuck and Bea

ADDITIONAL RESOURCES

Our Website: www.masscustomizedlearning.com

We are extending *Inevitable: Mass Customizing Learning* with our website created by our partners, Technology & Innovation in Education. TIE is a highly regarded not-for-profit service organization located in the Black Hills of South Dakota with values and goals that are very consistent with MASS CUSTOMIZED LEARNING. With a commitment to 21ˢᵗ Century teaching and learning and more than two decades of expertise with educational technologies, TIE is positioned as a national leader and a rich resource for progressive schools. TIE takes a systems view to providing services which are grounded in solid research and sound practices. School leaders and classroom teachers appreciate TIE's insights and practical approach for engaging today's students successfully.

The purpose of *www.masscutomizedlearning.com* is to:

- Inform . . . to make our profession aware of the **MCL** vision, its power and potential.
- Extend our learning . . . our learning about the **MCL** vision. *Inevitable* provides a very good start, but new insights will naturally follow.
- Share . . . we want to interact with dreamers and practitioners. No one of us is as smart as all of us.

MCL is a new, fresh, innovative vision that we believe will develop rapidly when people study, accept, and embrace a vision with the potential to customize learning for each learner. We will all learn as we go! We will all learn together!

To these ends, *www.masscustomizedlearning.com* quite naturally focuses on the study and implementation of MASS CUSTOMIZED LEARNING, but it also provides helpful information and resources on the following related topics.

Lori: The Video

Genius, talent and vision are a powerful equation. Geniuses at TIE have created a video of Chapter 7: *"Lori Does Her Learning Plan / Schedule."* It is a concrete picture of what **MCL** might look like at the high school level. Lori, of course, is an actress and the Lincoln Unlimited Learning Center does not exist - *YET*. However, currently there are schools and districts beginning their journey to becoming a **MCL** system. The Lori Video can be accessed on our website or on YouTube. Search "**MCL**: Lori Schedules Her Learning Plan."

Leadership

Schwahn is co-author of the AASA bestselling book titled _Total Leaders: Applying the Best Future-Focused Change Strategies to Education._

The Future

Your humble authors have written and continue to update a paper titled _The Future IS Now_ that is very useful in our time of rapid change.

Total Leaders Development

Training modules/materials based on thirteen critical Performance Roles of the Total Leader.

Book Reports

Power Point summaries of popular leadership, change, and futuristic books.

An "Inevitable Fieldbook" Appears to be Inevitable!

This new edition of _Inevitable_ provides your "still humble" authors an opportunity to thank readers for making the Inevitable Vision such a huge success. The near universal acceptance of the vision as exciting, desirable, and doable has been beyond our already high expectations. The buzz that the vision has created is most satisfying. Influencing change in education is our goal. More than ever, we think that education is poised for significant change . . . for transformational, reinvention kind of change. We have new hope for our profession!

The success of _Inevitable_ has given birth to an _Inevitable Fieldbook_ that will provide concrete steps that can be taken to begin personal and organizational movement toward the MASS CUSTOMIZED LEARNING vision. Our close colleagues and partners at TIE (Technology & Innovation in Education) are taking the lead in the creation of the _Inevitable Fieldbook_. Watch for "starter step" activities on TIE's website (www.tie.net) and on ours (www.masscustomizedlearning.

com). The hard copy fieldbook will be available before the beginning of the next school year. The *Inevitable Fieldbook*, which will be available from Amazon. com, will begin to answer your "how to" questions.

From Our Library

"Good artists copy.....great artists steal."

Picasso

With our deep respect, we thank the following thinkers and geniuses who continue to expand, challenge, and motivate our thinking.

Anderson, C. (2009). *Free.* New York: Hyperion.

Barker, J. (1988). *Discovering the Future: The Business of Paradigms.* St. Paul, MN: ILI Press.

Bossiy, L. and R. Charan. (2004). *Confronting Reality.* New York: Crown Business.

Bridges, W. (1991). *Managing Transitions.* Reading, MA: Addison-Wesley.

Christenson, C. (2008). *Disrupting Class.* New York: McGraw-Hill.

Christenson, C., and S. Anthony, E. Roth. (2004). *Seeing What's Next.* Boston: Harvard Business School Publishing.

Collins, J. (2001). *Good To Great.* New York: Harper Collins.

Covington, Martin (1998). *The Will To Learn: A Guide for Motivating Young People.* Cambridge University Press.

Deci, Edward L. (1995). *Why We Do What We Do: Understanding Self-Motivation.* Penguin Books.

DuFour, R. and R. DuFour, R. Eaker, and G. Karhanek. (2004). *Whatever It Takes: How Professional Learning Communities Respond When Kids Don't Learn.* Solution Tree.

Dweck, Carol S. (2006). *Mindset: The New Psychology of Success.* New York: Ballantine Books.

Gardner, H. (2006). *Five Minds for the Future.* Boston: Harvard Business School Press.

Goleman, Daniel (1998). *Working With Emotional Intelligence.* Bantam Books.

Heath, Chip and Dan Heath (2007). *Make To Stick.* Random House.

Heath, Chip and Dan Heath (2010). *Switch: How To Change Things When Change Is Hard.* Random House

Johnson, S. (2002). *Who Moved My Cheese*. Vermillion.

Kelly, F. and T. McCain, I. Jukes. (2008). *Teaching the Digital Generation*. Crown Press.

Kotter, J.P. (2008). *A Sense of Urgency*. Boston: Harvard Business School Press.

Kubler-Ross, E. (1969). *On Death And Dying*. New York: Macmillan Publishing Company.

Palfrey, J and U. Glasser. (2009). *Born Digital*. New York: Basic Books.

Peters, Tom (2003). *Re-imagine*. Dorling Kindersley.

Pink D. (2009). *Drive*. New York: Riverhead Books.

Robinson, K. (2009). *The Element*. Viking Adult.

Schwahn, C. and W. G. Spady, (2002). *Total Leaders: Applying the Best Future-Focused Change Strategies to Education*. Rowman and Littlefield.

Schwahn, C. and W. G. Spady. (2010). *Total Leaders 2.0: Leading in the Age of Empowerment*. New York: Rowman and Littlefield.

Shirky, C. (2008). *Here Comes Everybody*. New York: The Penguin Press.

Spady, W. G. (2001). *Beyond Counterfeit Reforms*. Boston: Scarecrow Press.

_____, (1994). *Outcome Based Education*. Arlington, VA: American Association of School Administrators.

Spady, W. G. and C. Schwahn (2010). *Learning Communities 2.0*. New York: Rowman and Littlefield.

Stoddard, L (2008). *Educating for Human Greatness*. Brandon, VT: Holistic Education Press.

Tapscott, D. (2008). *Grown Up Digital*. New York: McGraw-Hill.

Tapscott, D. and A. Williams. (2006). *Wikinomics: How Mass Collaboration Changes Everything*. New York: Times Books.

Vander Ark, Tom (2011). *Getting Smart: How Digital Learning is Changing the World*. San Francisco: Josey-Bass.

OUR THANKS

Writing *Inevitable* has been work that was actually a bit painful at times for two people who would rather talk, read, and listen than write. But it has also been fun and rewarding. We have long wanted to put our vision of **MCL** into book form. Although we feel the book is truly ours, we did steal/borrow from many of our heroes and heroines. We have learned so much from so many that it has become difficult to determine from whom we first learned a specific skill, concept, or strategy. When speaking to groups we frequently begin by cleverly stating, "to steal intellectual property from an individual is plagiarism . . . but to steal from everyone is research."

Our learning, our perspective, and our work have roots in leadership, change, and future-focused strategic design literature. We have been mentored . . . from a distance . . . by gurus Ken Blanchard, Tom Peters, Margaret Wheatley, Marcus Buckingham, Rosabeth Moss Kanter, Stephen Covey, Tom Friedman, Daniel Goleman, Daniel Pink, Jack Welch, Elizabeth Kubler-Ross, Ken Robinson, Chip and Dan Heath, and 50+ others whose books decorate our shelves.

But given that our life missions are firmly grounded in education, we acknowledge that our beliefs, values, and strategies have been significantly influenced by our educational gurus – Larry Lezotte, Bill Spady, Bob Marzano, Madeline Hunter, Edward Deci, John Hattie, Martin Covington, Richard Mayer, and Marc Prensky. As with our leadership gurus, this list could also go on and on. We stand on their shoulders.

More specifically, many good friends and trusted colleagues have read the beta version of *Inevitable* and provided valuable feedback. Big thanks to our friends and colleagues Pat Crawford, Debra Pickering, Jay Scott, Mary Esposito, Harold Ferguson, Mary McDonough, Charollene Coates, Jim Keckler, Tom LaFavore, and Vicki Shannon. We appreciated your feedback and your suggestions, but mostly we were kept motivated by your confirmations and support.

Getting closer to home . . . actually getting into our homes . . . we must thank our mates we jokingly referred to as "our staff." Genny, Chuck's bride, has been first editor, grammarian, proofer, encourager, supporter, nudger, and all around good girl. Thank goodness I (Chuck) had the foresight to "cross train my staff." Richard, Bea's favorite guy, has been her indispensable on-site coach, mentor, and questioner. The "atta-girls" were plentiful with an occasional (and necessary) "cowgirl-up." Through the entire process of creating *Inevitable: Mass*

Customized Learning we did receive a few grievances from "our staff" . . . but none that got to the "formal hearing" stage.

And finally, a large "thank you" to each other. We began our writing project based upon our common mission and our solid personal and professional relationship. That relationship has been enhanced and strengthened through our collaborative work. We are closer friends and more supportive colleagues because of our collaboration. And that's how it should be when all is well.